# Unbelievably CUTE ORIGAMI

by Tatsukuri Origami

## Table of Contents

Tatsukuri's Origami Gallery ........ 2
Basic Origami Techniques
 & Symbols ........ 14
Tips for Drawing Faces
 & Markings ........ 42

### ◆ CUTE PETS ........ 2
Shiba Inu ........ 16
Pug ........ 19
Toy Poodle ........ 22
Relaxed Cat ........ 24
Rabbit ........ 26
Heart Hamster ........ 29

### ◆ LIVELY ZOO ANIMALS ........ 4
Lion ........ 32
Elephant ........ 35
Gorilla ........ 38
Panda ........ 40
Tiger ........ 43
Tree, Leaves & Grass ........ 46

### ◆ FRIENDLY FOREST ANIMALS ........ 6
Fox ........ 48
Mole ........ 50
Hedgehog ........ 52
Owl ........ 54
Squirrel ........ 56
Japanese Snow Fairy ........ 59
Bumblebee ........ 60

### ◆ COOL AQUATIC & WATERSIDE ANIMALS ........ 8
Dolphin ........ 62
Whale ........ 64
Penguin ........ 66
Polar Bear ........ 68
Otter ........ 70
Frog ........ 72

### ◆ ANIMAL MODELS FOR CELEBRATIONS ........ 10
Rabbit Dolls (*Usabina*) ........ 75
Easter Bunny ........ 78
Halloween Costumes ........ 80
Chimney Cat ........ 82
Santa's-Boot Cat ........ 84
Reindeer ........ 86
Full-Moon Rabbit ........ 89

### ◆ PRACTICAL ANIMAL ORIGAMI MODELS ........ 12
Rabbit Chopstick Holder ........ 90
Cat Bookmark ........ 92
Cat (or Bear) Envelope ........ 94
Cat (or Bear) Message Card ........ 95

Tatsukuri Origami is on YouTube! ........ 96

> **About the Origami Paper Used to Fold These Models**
> In this book, we mainly call for using 6 × 6-in (15 × 15-cm) origami paper (measured edge to edge). In some cases, smaller sizes are called for, but if you find these difficult to fold, try using paper larger than 6 in (15 cm). All origami paper called for is square unless otherwise indicated.

**TUTTLE** Publishing

Tokyo | Rutland, Vermont | Singapore

# CUTE PETS

▶ Tatsukuri's Origami Gallery

**Relaxed Cats** ▶ page 24

We're so cute!

**Heart Hamsters** ▶ page 29

**Rabbits** ▶ page 26

# LIVELY ZOO ANIMALS

Leaves ▶ page 46
Lion ▶ page 32
Trees ▶ page 46
Tigers ▶ page 43
Elephants ▶ page 35
Grass ▶ page 46

▶ Tatsukuri's Origami Gallery

Gorillas ▶ page 38

Pandas ▶ page 40

# FRIENDLY FOREST ANIMALS

Squirrels ▸ page 56

What's the buzz?

Bumblebees ▸ page 60

Fox ▸ page 48

Moles ▸ page 50

Trees ▸ page 46

Leaves ▸ page 46

Tatsukuri's Origami Gallery

Hedgehogs ▶ page 52

We're tiny but spiny!

Owls ▶ page 54

Tree ▶ page 46

Japanese Snow Fairy ▶ page 59

# COOL AQUATIC & WATERSIDE ANIMALS

Dolphins ▶ page 62

Whales ▶ page 64

▶ Tatsukuri's Origami Gallery

Penguins ▶ page 66

Does anyone else have cold feet?

Polar Bear ▶ page 68

Frogs ▶ page 72

Otters ▶ page 70

May we have fish for lunch today?

9

# ANIMAL MODELS FOR CELEBRATIONS

Doll Festival (*Hinamatsuri*)

Rabbit Dolls (*Usabina*) ▶ page 75

Easter

Easter Bunny ▶ page 78

It's fun to fold using papers with different patterns!

▶ Tatsukuri's Origami Gallery

**Moon Viewing Festival**

Full-Moon Rabbit ▶ page 89

**Halloween**

Halloween Costumes ▶ page 80

Tiger Costume

Fox Costume

**Christmas**

Santa's-Boot Cat ▶ page 84

Chimney Cat ▶ page 82

Reindeer ▶ page 86

# PRACTICAL ANIMAL ORIGAMI MODELS

Rabbit Chopstick Holders ▶ page 90

Cat (or Bear) Envelopes ▶ page 94

Cat Envelopes     Bear Envelopes

▶ Tatsukuri's Origami Gallery

Cat Bookmarks ▶ page 92

Cat (or Bear) Message Cards ▶ page 95

# Basic Origami Techniques & Symbols
An explanation of the folding methods and symbols used in this book

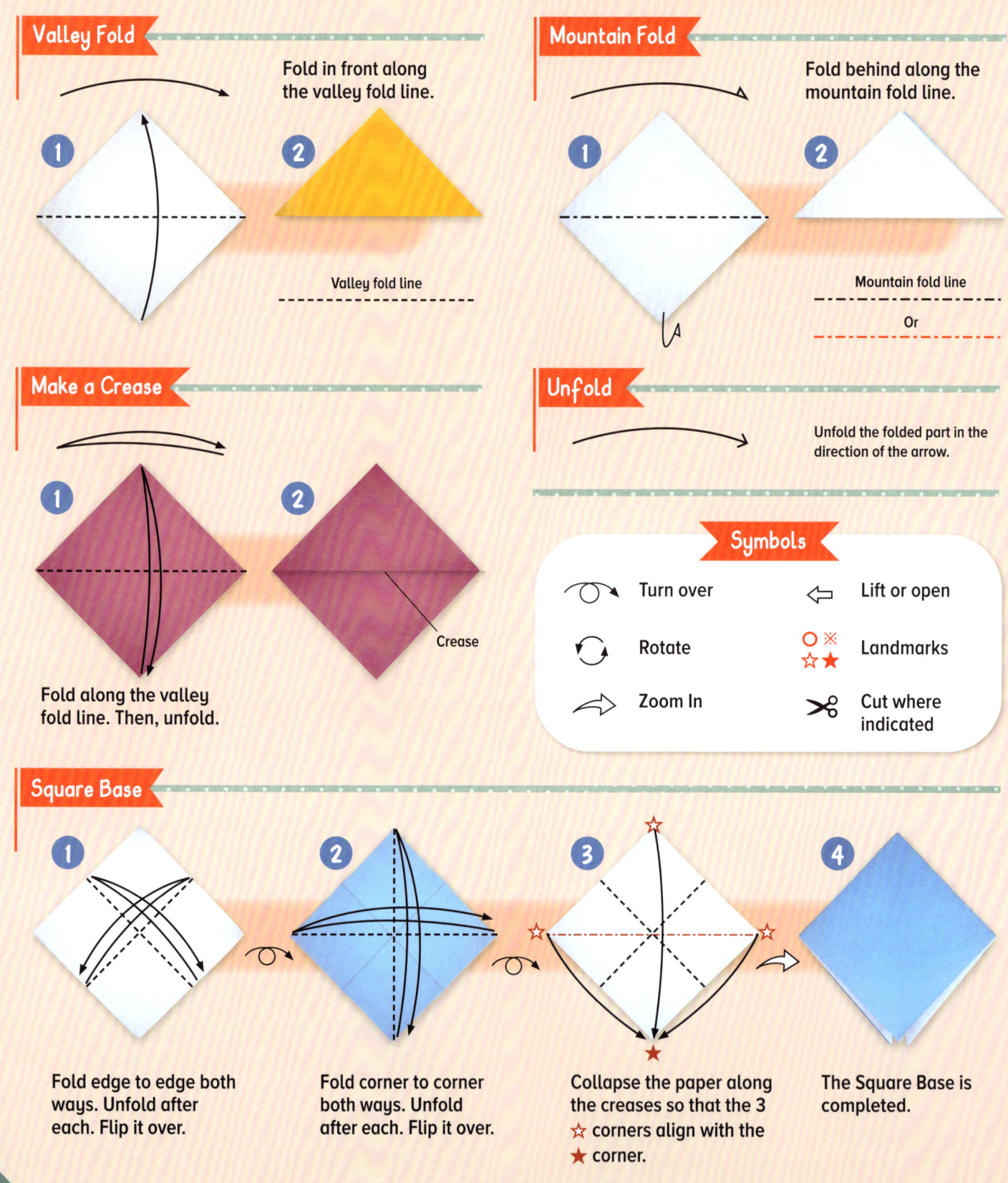

## Waterbomb Base

**1** Fold edge to edge both ways. Unfold after each. Flip it over.

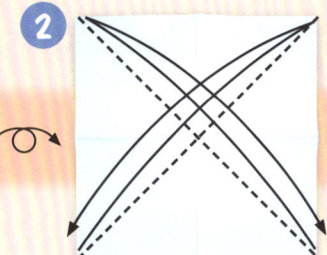
**2** Fold corner to corner both ways. Unfold after each.

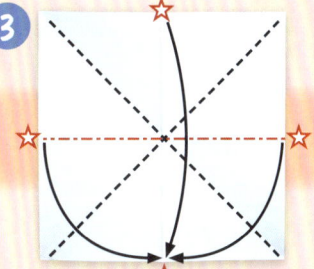
**3** Collapse the paper along the creases so that the 3 ☆ locations align with the ★ location.

**4** The Waterbomb Base is completed.

## Inside Reverse Fold

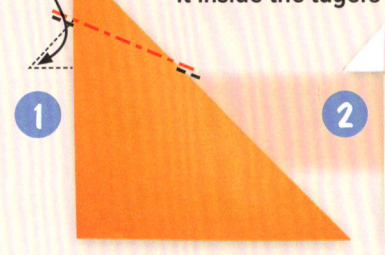
Fold the corner inward, tucking it inside the layers of paper.

## Step Fold

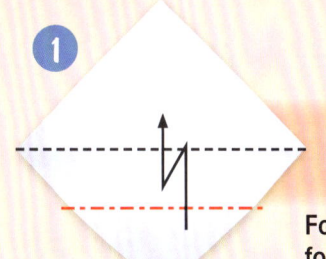
Fold using mountain and valley folds to create a stepped shape.

## Useful Tools

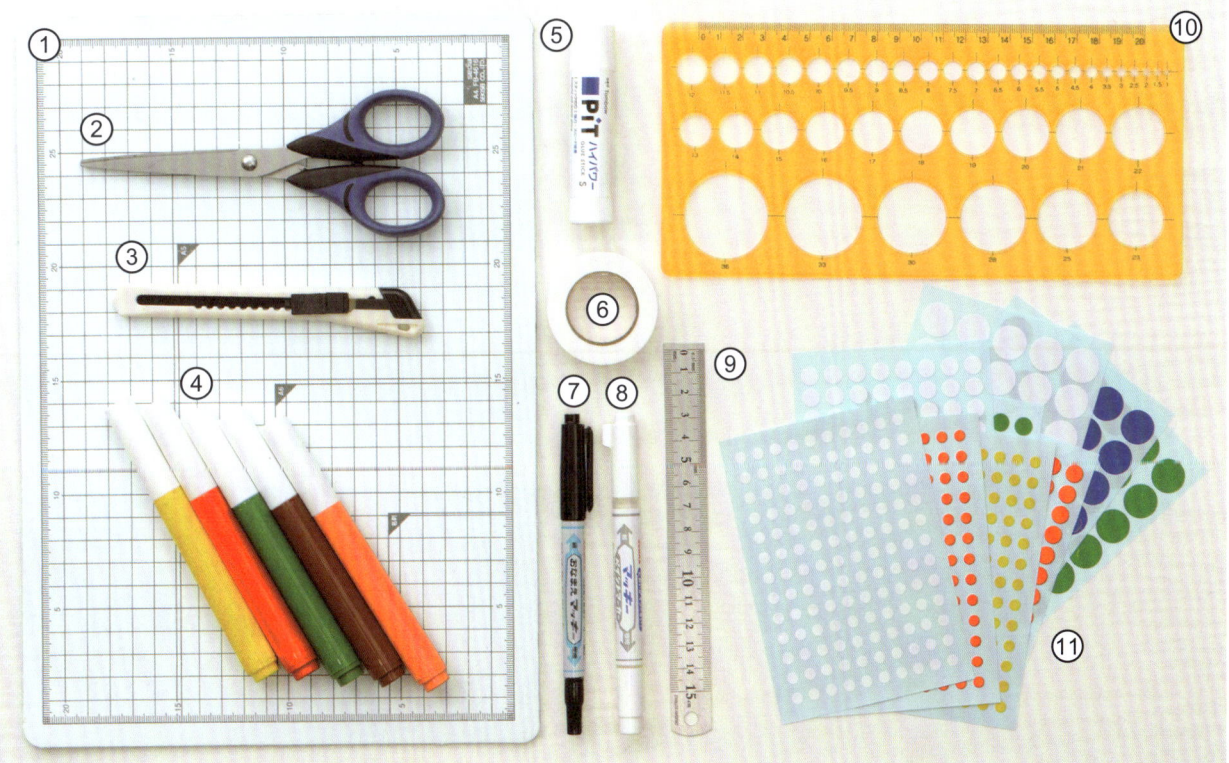

① Cutting mat
② Scissors
③ Craft knife
④ Markers
⑤ Glue stick
⑥ Masking tape
⑦ Black felt tip pen
⑧ White paint pen
⑨ Ruler
⑩ Circle template
⑪ **Various round stickers** (Instructions for using round stickers are on page 42, "Tips for Drawing Faces & Markings")

▶ Cute Pets

# Shiba Inu
▶ Photo on page 2

I'm made from two parts, so I can have realistic two-tone color!

Standing Version · Flat Version

▶ **Origami paper to use:** Head: One 6-in (15-cm) sheet / Body: One 6-in (15-cm) sheet
▶ **Recommended tools:** Black felt tip pen, white paint pen

## 🚩 Head

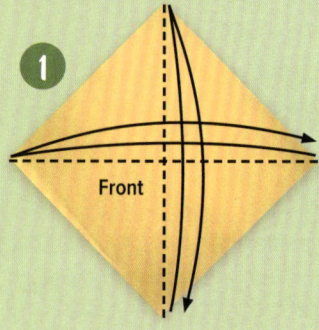

**1** Fold corner to corner both ways. Unfold after each.

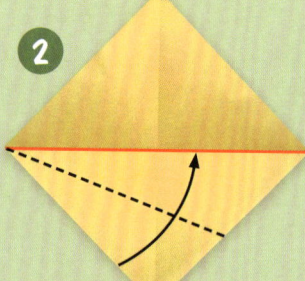

**2** Fold the edge to align with the crease.

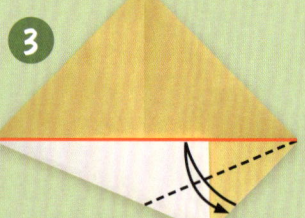

**3** Fold the other edge to align with the crease. Unfold.

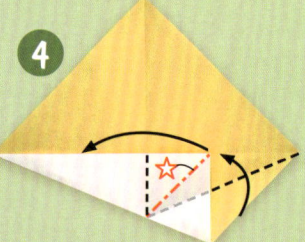

**4** Pinch along the ☆ crease and fold the flap to the left.

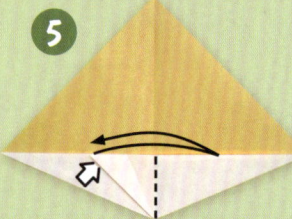

**5** Fold the flap to the right to make a crease. Unfold.

**6** Fold the edge along the existing crease to reinforce it. Unfold.

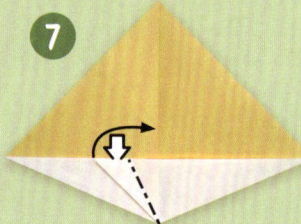

**7** Open up the pocket and squash it flat.

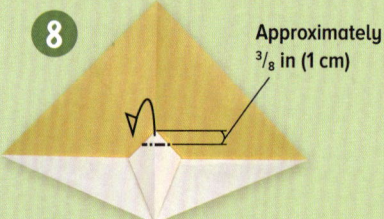

**8** Mountain fold the corner at the position shown in the diagram. Approximately 3/8 in (1 cm)

**9** This is the result. Flip it over.

**10** Fold the corner to the intersection of creases.

**11** Fold the corner to the bottom edge.

**12** Fold the corner to the top edge. Unfold.

16

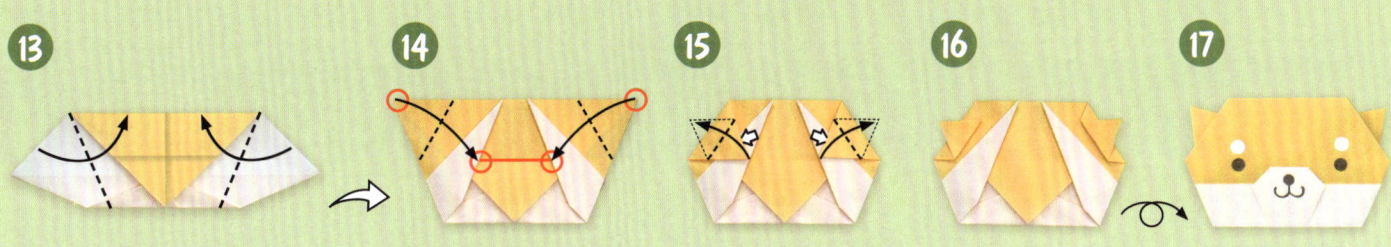

**13** Fold the edges up to align with the top edge.

**14** Fold so that the paired ○ points meet.

**15** Fold the corners so that they protrude a little to either side.

**16** Step 15 is completed. Flip it over.

**17** Draw the face to complete the Head.

## Body (Standing Version)

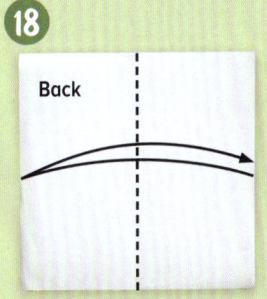
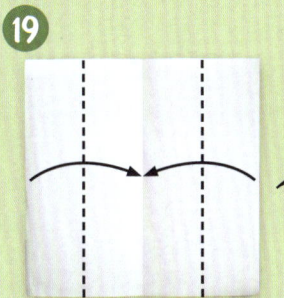
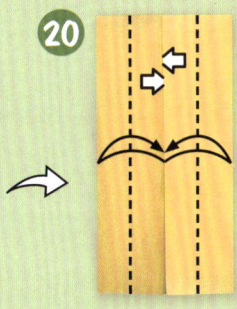
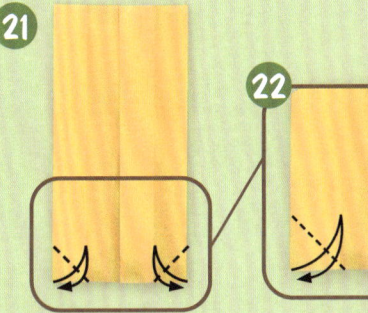
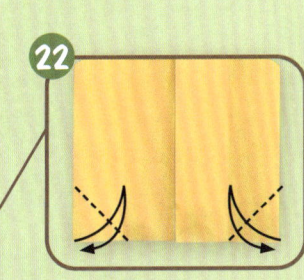

**18** Fold the paper in half edge to edge. Unfold.

**19** Fold the edges to align with the crease.

**20** Fold the edges of the flaps to the outside edges. Unfold both.

**21** Fold the corners to meet the step-20 creases. Unfold both.

**22** Enlarged view.

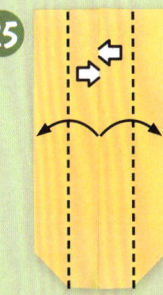

**23** Inside reverse fold the corners along the creases from step 21.

**24** Step 23 is completed.

**25** Fold the flaps out using the step-20 creases.

**26** Step 25 is completed. Flip it over.

**27** This is how it looks flipped over.

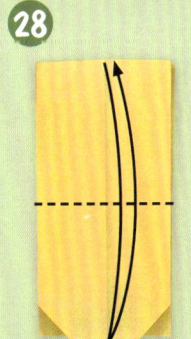

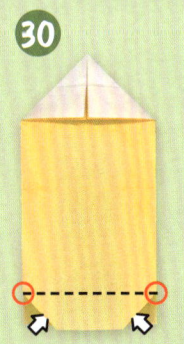
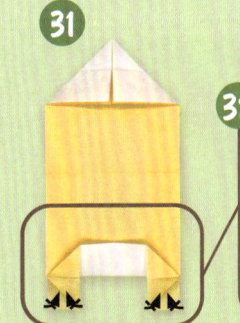

**28** Fold edge to edge. Unfold.

**29** Fold the corners to meet the vertical crease.

**30** Fold the flap up along the ○-to-○ span.

**31** Fold in small portions of all 4 corners.

**32** Enlarged view.

**33** Step 31 is completed.

17

▶ Cute Pets

# Pug
▶ Photo on page 2

VIDEO:
tuttlepublishing.com/
unbelievably-cute-origami

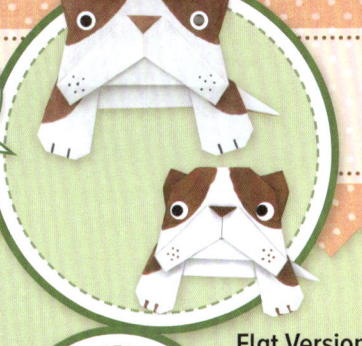

Decorate me by drawing polka dots and other patterns on my face and body.

Flat Version

Standing Version

- **Origami paper to use:** Head (Large): One 6-in (15-cm) sheet / Body (Large): One 6-in (15-cm) sheet; Head (Small): One 4¾-in (12-cm) sheet / Body (Small): One 4¾-in (12-cm) sheet
- **Recommended tools:** Black felt tip pen, markers, round stickers (white, 5/16 in / 8 mm; black, 3/16 in / 5 mm), glue or masking tape
→ The following instructions show 6-in (15-cm) origami paper being used.

## Head

**1**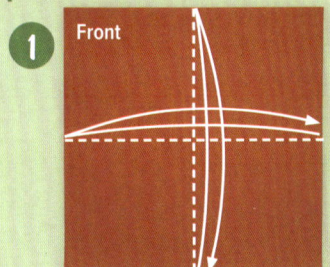
Fold edge to edge both ways. Unfold after each.

**2**
Fold the bottom corners to the center. Unfold both.

**3**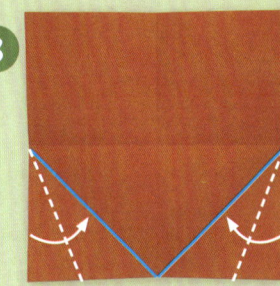
Fold the edges to meet the step-2 creases.

**4**
Fold the outside edges to meet the ☆-to-☆ edges.

**5**
Fold along the existing creases.

**6**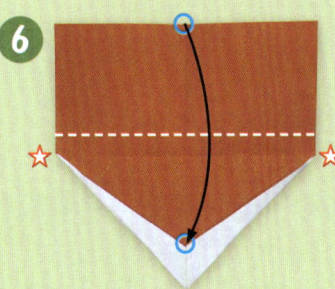
Fold so that the 2 ○ points meet.

**7**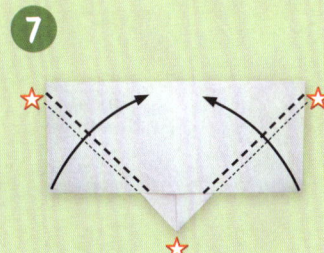
Fold slightly inside the diagonal edges (☆-to-☆) formed in step 5.

**8**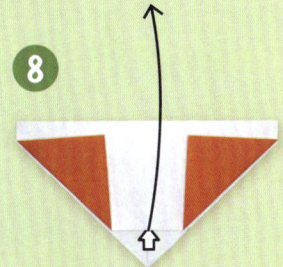
Open the paper and lift upward.

**9**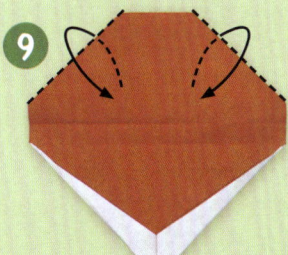
Re-fold the triangular flaps made in step 7 to the front side.

**10**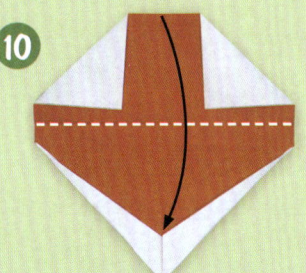
Fold along the existing crease.

**11**
Open the parts marked with ↗ and tuck the flap from step 10 inside.

**12**
Step 11 is completed. Flip it over.

**13** Fold the corner to the crease.

**14** Fold down a small portion of the corner.

**15** This is the result. Flip it over.

**16** Starting from the lower right corner (↖), open up the paper and fold it down. Bring the — and — edge portions together.

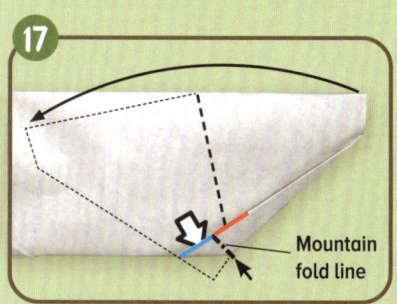

**17** Enlarged view of step 16.

**18** Fold in a small portion of the upper right corner.

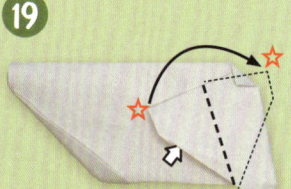

**19** Fold back so that point ☆ protrudes slightly at the upper right—this will become the ear.

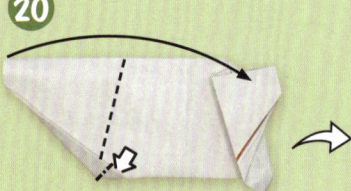

**20** Fold the left side in mirror image to steps 16–17.

**21** Fold in a small portion of the upper left corner.

**22** Fold the same manner as in step 19.

**23** This is the result. Flip it over.

**24** Draw the nose and whisker patterns, color in the coat markings and apply the round stickers—the Head is completed!

## Body (Standing Version)

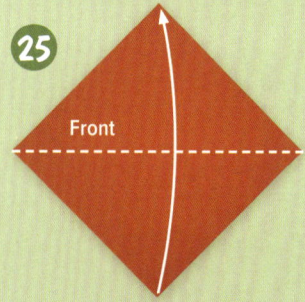

**25** Fold the paper in half corner to corner.

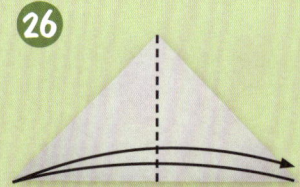

**26** Fold corner to corner. Unfold.

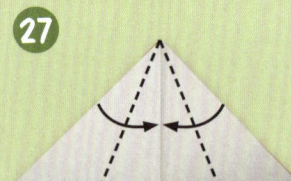

**27** Fold the edges to align with the crease.

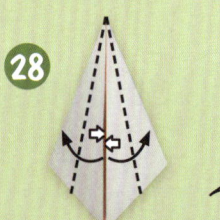

**28** Fold the edges in the center out to align with the outside edges.

**29** Step 28 is completed. Flip it over.

**30** This is how it looks flipped over.

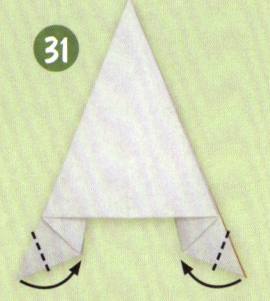
**31** Fold corner to corner on both sides.

**32** Fold small portions of the corners up.

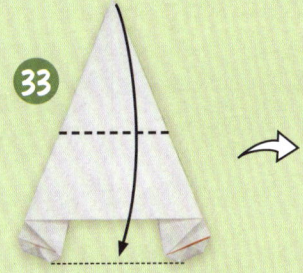
**33** Fold the top corner down to the midpoint of the span between the lowest points.

**34** This is the result. Flip it over.

**35** Draw the pattern to complete the Body (Standing Version).

**36** *Completed* — Attach the Head to complete the Standing Version.

## Body (Flat Version)

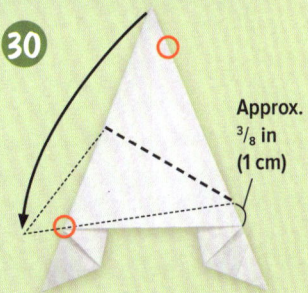
**30** Starting from step 30 of the Standing Version, fold so that the 2 ○ points meet. Approx. 3/8 in (1 cm)

**31** Fold the outside edge in to bisect the angle of the flap as shown.

**32** Tuck the corner folded in step 31 inside.

**33** Fold corner to corner on both sides.

**34** Fold small portions of the corners up.

**35** Step 34 is completed. Flip it over.

**36** Color in the coat markings to complete the Body (Flat Version).

**37** *Completed* — Attach the Head to complete the Flat Version.

21

▶ Cute Pets

# Toy Poodle
▶ Photo on page 2

VIDEO:
tuttlepublishing.com/
unbelievably-cute-origami

"I'm made with two parts. You can also stand me up for display."

Flat Version

Standing Version

- **Origami paper to use:** Head: One 6-in (15-cm) sheet / Body: One 6-in (15-cm) sheet
- **Recommended tools:** Black felt tip pen, white paint pen, round stickers (black, 5/16 in / 8 mm)

## ⚑ Head

**1**
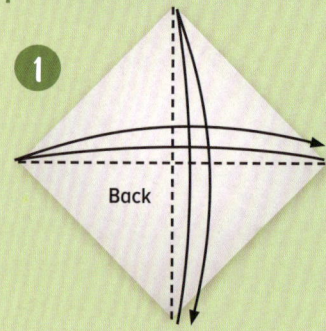
Fold corner to corner both ways. Unfold after each.

**2**
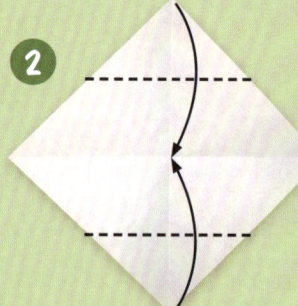
Fold both corners to the center.

**3**

Refold along the existing crease.

**4**
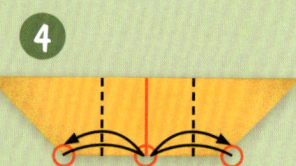
Fold the obtuse-angle corners to the center to create new creases. Unfold both.

**5**
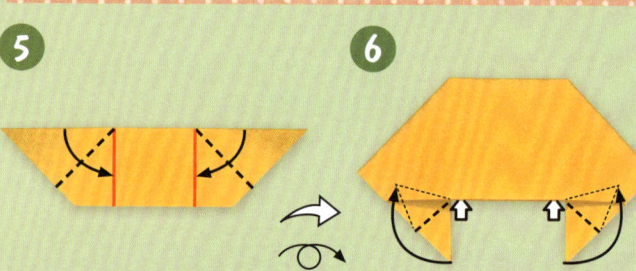
Fold segments of the top edge down to align with the step-4 creases. Flip it over.

**6**
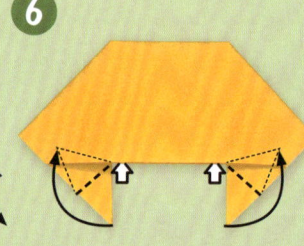
Fold the bottom corners and then partially open the paper to tuck them inside.

**7**

Fold the outside corners at the indicated positions. Flip the paper over.

**8**
Use a pen or round stickers for the eyes

Draw the muzzle and apply eye stickers to finish the Head.

## ⚑ Body (Standing Version)

**9**
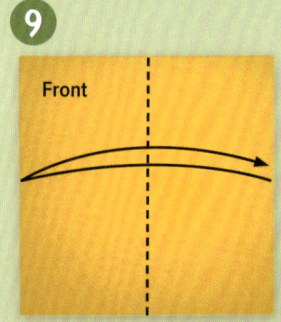
Fold the paper in half edge to edge. Unfold.

**10**
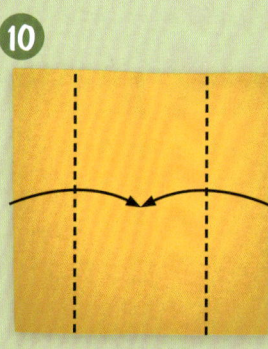
Fold the edges to align with the crease.

**11**
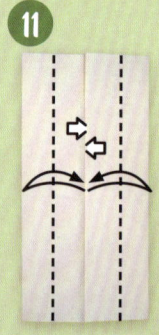
Fold the edges of the flaps to the outside edges. Unfold both.

**12**
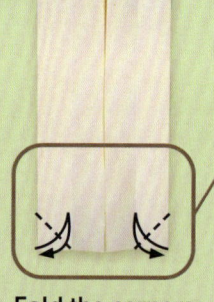
Fold the corners to meet the step-11 creases. Unfold both.

**13**
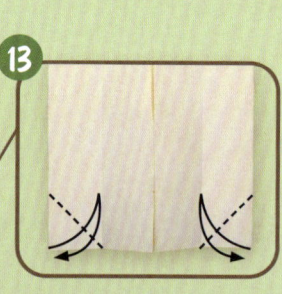
Enlarged view.

**14** Inside reverse fold the corners along the creases from step 12.

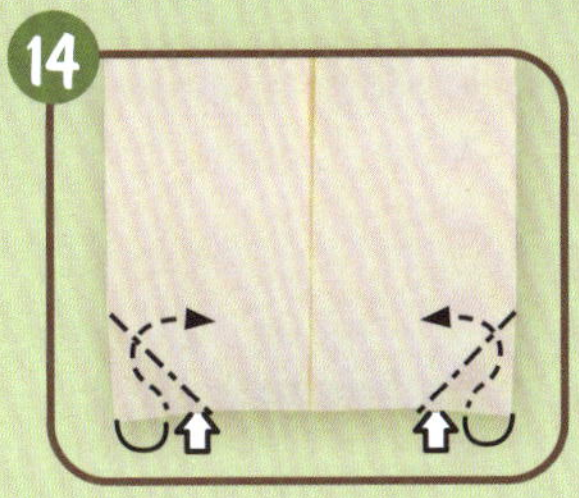

**15** Step 14 is completed.

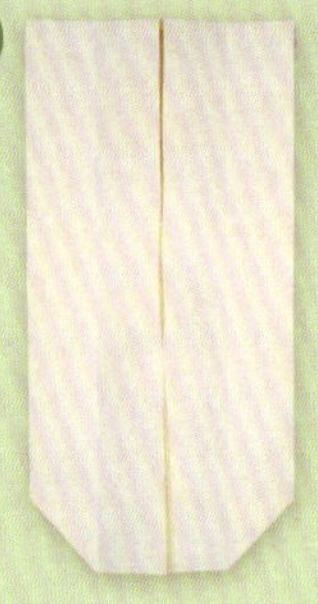

**16** Fold the flaps out using the step-11 creases.

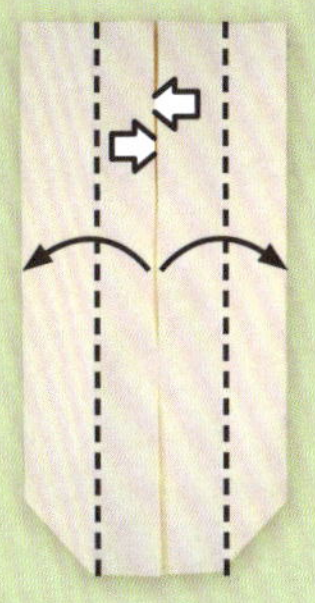

**17** Step 16 is completed. Flip it over.

**18** This is how it looks flipped over.

**19** Fold edge to edge. Unfold.

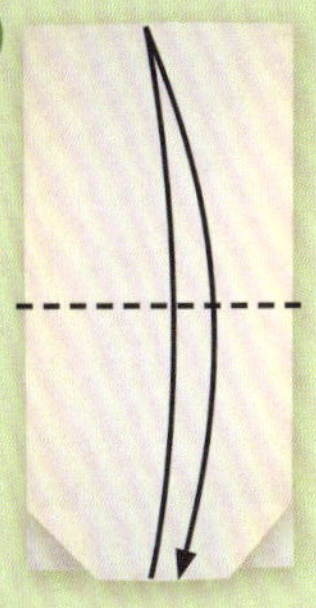

**20** Fold the corners to meet the vertical crease.

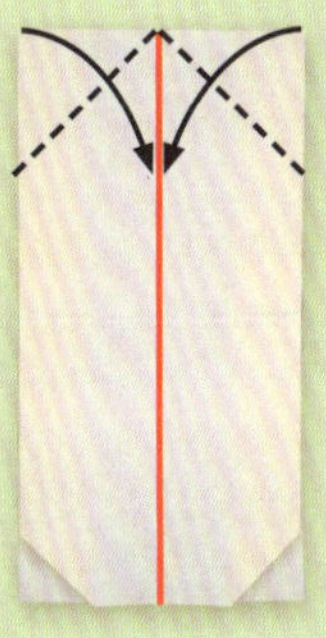

**21** Fold the flap up along the ○-to-○ span.

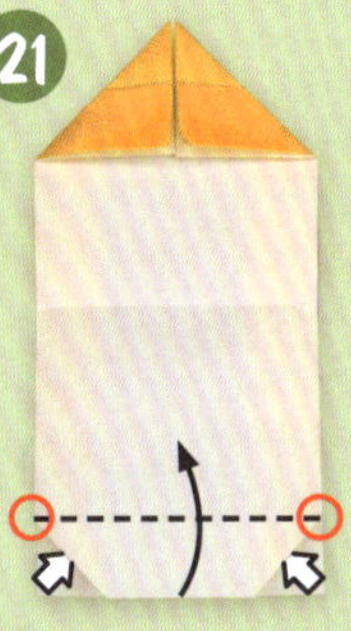

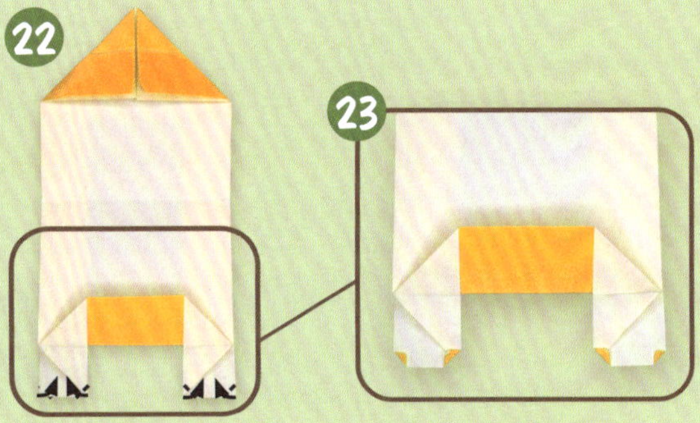

**22** Fold in small portions of all 4 corners.

**23** Enlarged view of completed step 22.

**24** Fold the top corner down to the midpoint of the span between the lowest points.

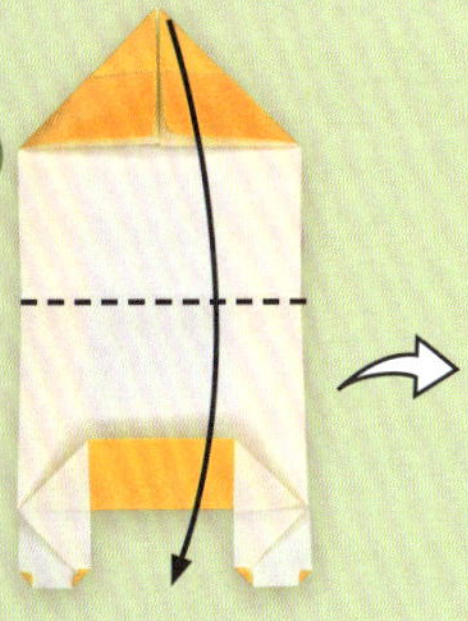

**25** This is the result. Flip it over.

**26** The Body (Standing Version) is completed.

**27** *Completed* Insert the Body into the pocket in the Head. The Standing Version is completed.

## Body (Flat Version)

**18** Starting from step 18 of the Standing Version, fold the flap along the ○-to-○ span. Unfold.

**19** Fold the top edge down to the crease.

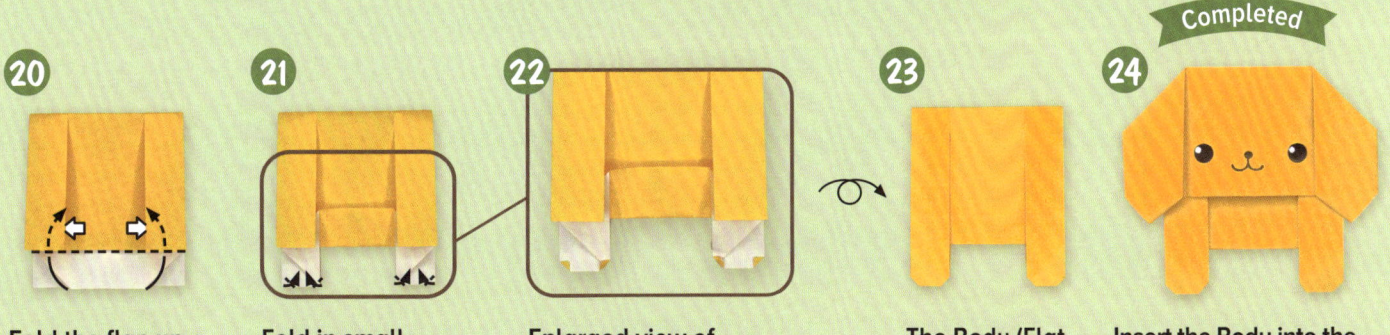

**20** Fold the flap up and tuck it inside on both sides.

**21** Fold in small portions of all 4 corners.

**22** Enlarged view of completed step 21.

**23** The Body (Flat Version) is completed.

**24** *Completed* Insert the Body into the pocket in the Head. The Flat Version is completed.

23

# Cute Pets

# Relaxed Cat
▶ Photo on page 3

VIDEO:
tuttlepublishing.com/
unbelievably-cute-origami

You can fold me from one sheet of paper. My relaxed pose is just irresistible!

It can also stand up

- **Origami paper to use:** One 6-in (15-cm) sheet
- **Recommended tools:** Black felt tip pen, white paint pen, markers, round stickers (black, 3/16 in / 5 mm)

## ▶ Tail-Out Version

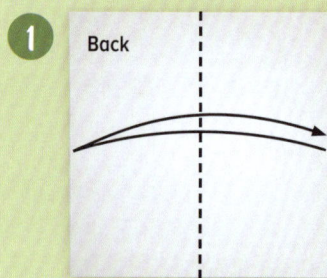

**1** Fold the paper in half edge to edge. Unfold.

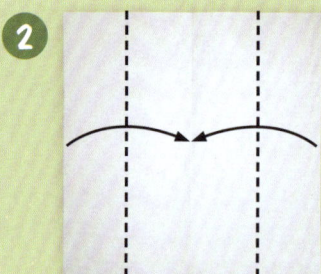

**2** Fold the edges to align with the crease. Flip it over.

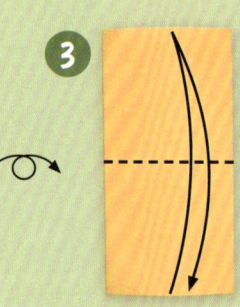

**3** Fold edge to edge. Unfold. Flip it over.

**4** Fold the corners to meet the center slit. Unfold both.

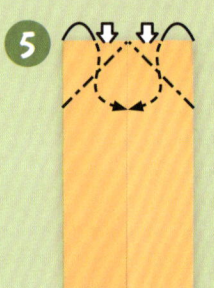

**5** Inside reverse fold the corners.

**6** Step 5 in progress.

**7** Step 5 is completed.

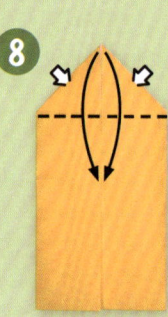

**8** Fold down the 2 flaps.

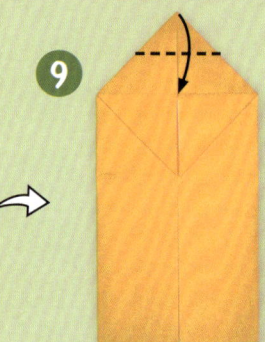

**9** Fold the corner down to meet the crease.

**10** Fold the triangular flaps up at an angle to form the ears.

**11** Step 10 is completed.

**12** Step fold so that the paired ○ points meet.

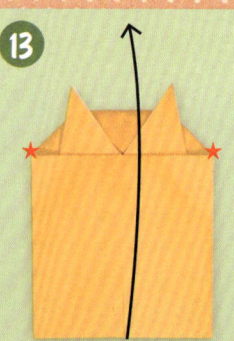

**13** Swing the flap up along the span between the ★ marks.

**14** Step 13 is completed.

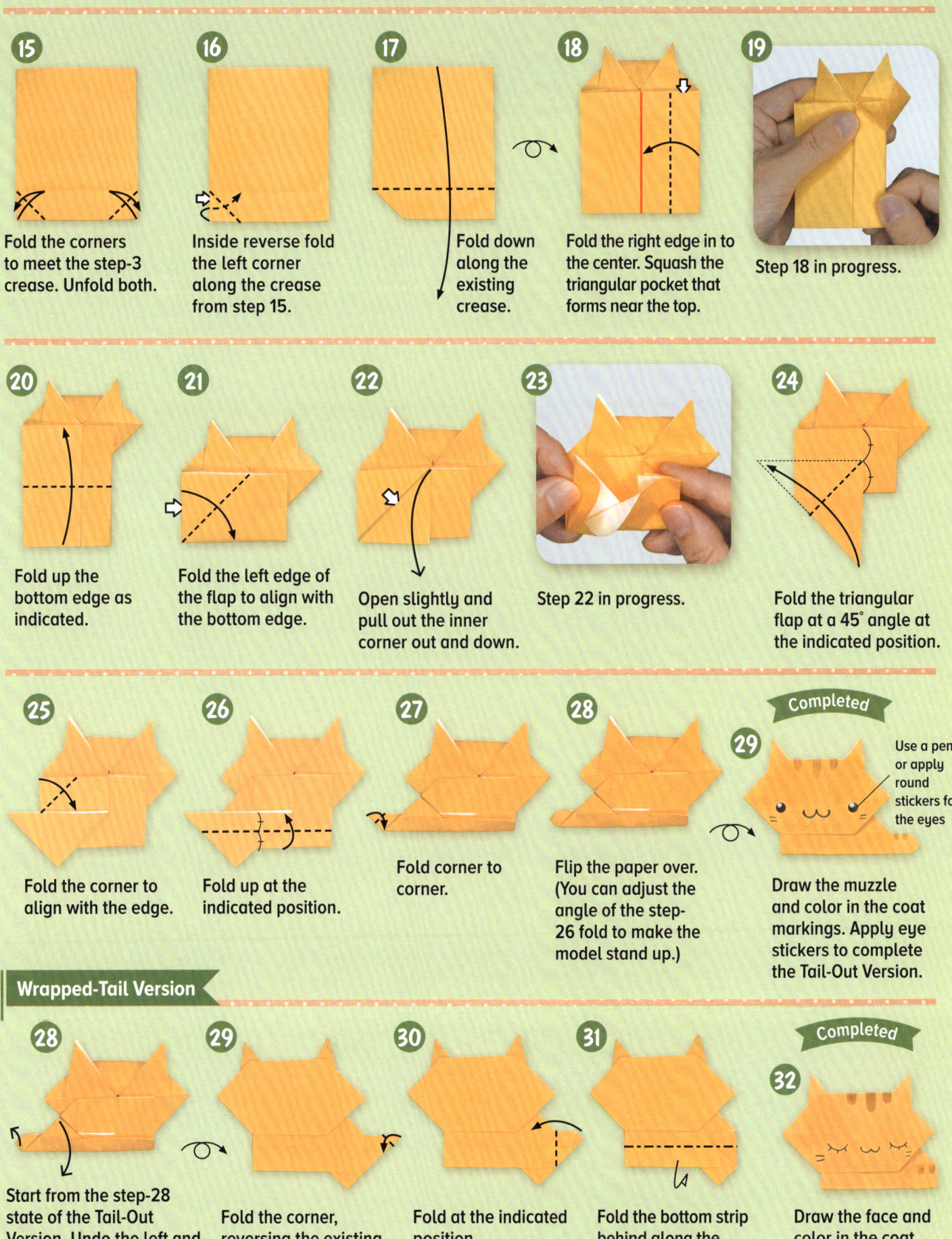

▶ Cute Pets

# Rabbit
▶ Photo on page 3

VIDEO:
tuttlepublishing.com/
unbelievably-cute-origami

I'm folded from two sheets of origami paper. My long ears are amazing!

- **Origami paper to use:** Head: One 6-in (15-cm) sheet / Body: One 3-in (7.5-cm) sheet
- **Recommended tools:** Black felt tip pen, markers, glue or masking tape

## Head

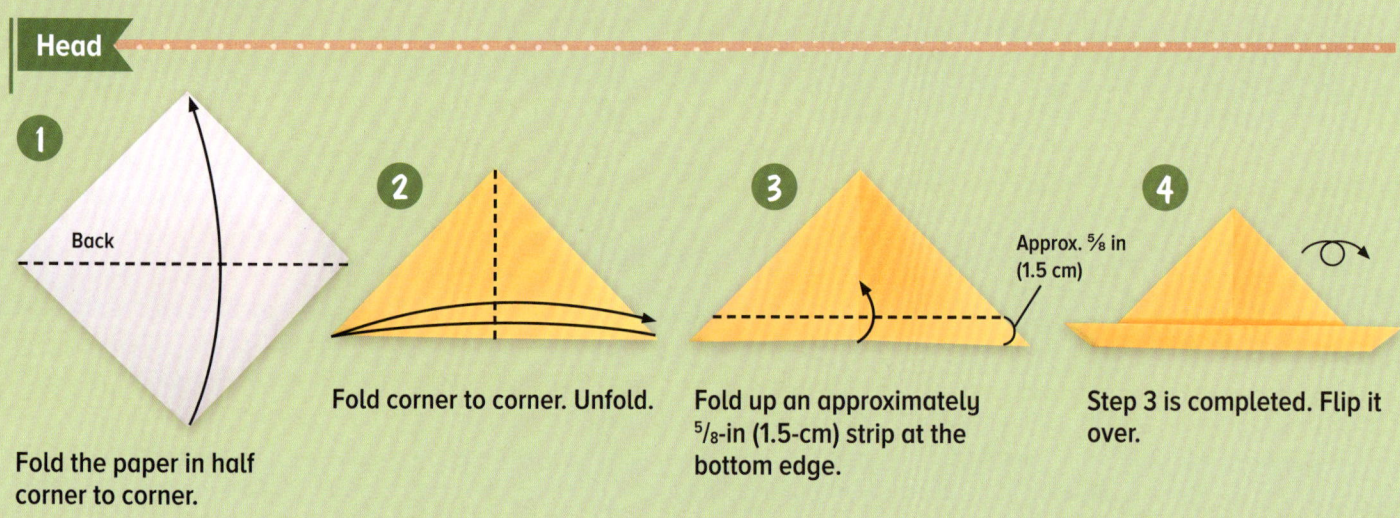

**1** Fold the paper in half corner to corner.

**2** Fold corner to corner. Unfold.

**3** Fold up an approximately 5/8-in (1.5-cm) strip at the bottom edge.

**4** Step 3 is completed. Flip it over.

**5** Fold up again using the same strip width as in step 3.

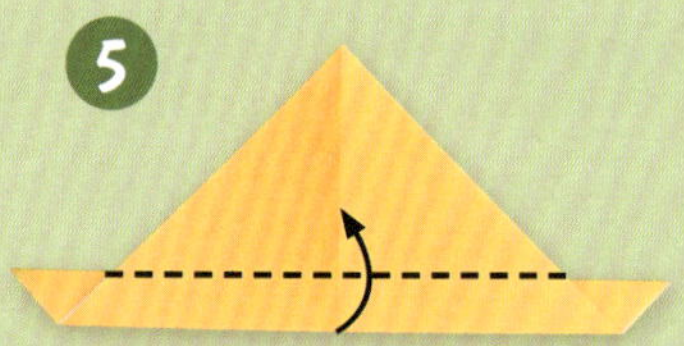

**6** Fold equal segments of the bottom edge up to align with the central vertical crease.

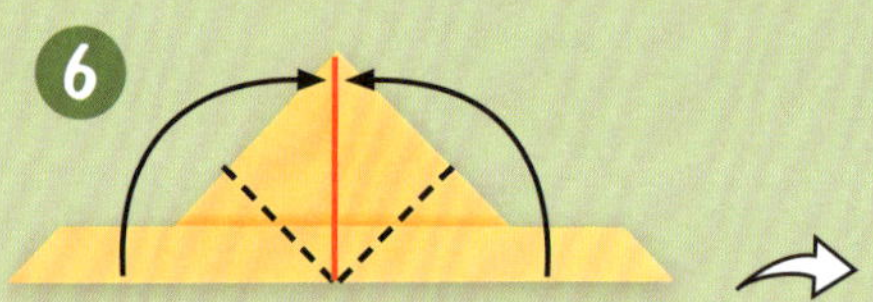

**7** Fold up the bottom corner at approximately 5/8 in (1.5 cm) from the tip.

**8** Return to the state at the beginning of step 6.

**9** Step 8 is completed.

**10** Fold along the crease.

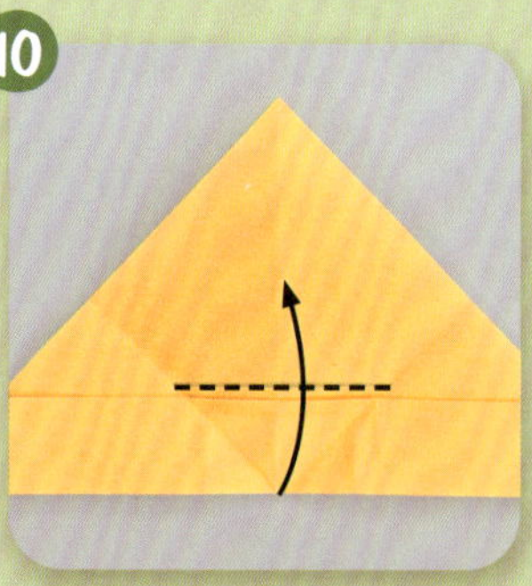

**11** Reverse the crease directions.

**12** Step 10 in progress.

26

**13** Fold both flaps corner to corner.

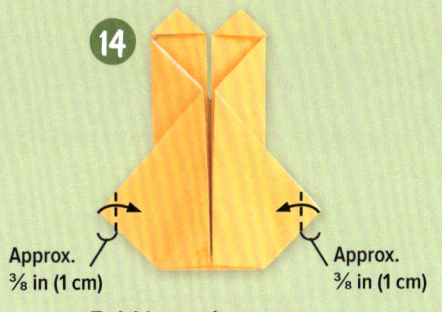
**14** Fold in each corner at about ⅜ in (1 cm) from the tip.

**15** Step 14 is completed. Flip it over.

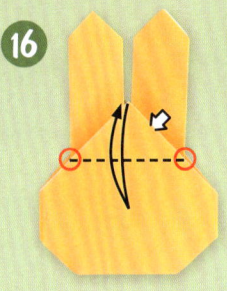
**16** Fold through both layers of the flap along the ○-to-○ span. Unfold.

🚩 Body

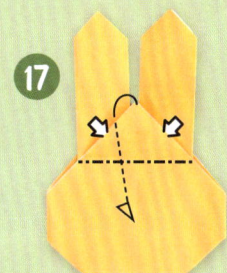
**17** Fold behind along the existing crease to tuck the flap inside.

**18** Draw on the face, and then the Head is completed.

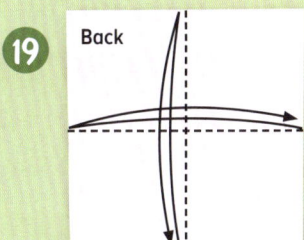
**19** Fold edge to edge both ways. Unfold after each.

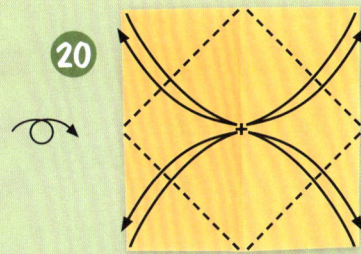
**20** Fold each corner to the center. Unfold each.

**21** Step 20 is completed. Flip it over.

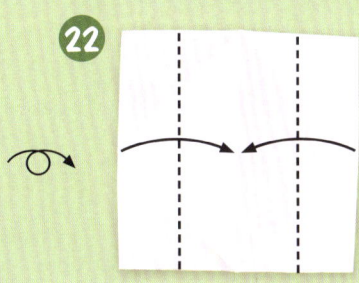
**22** Fold the edges to align with the vertical crease.

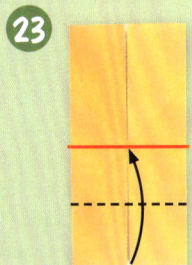
**23** Fold the bottom edge to the center.

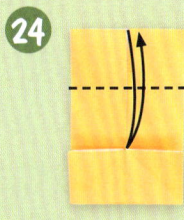
**24** Fold the top edge to the center. Unfold.

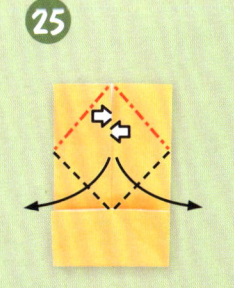
**25** Open along the diagonal creases and fold flat.

**26** Step 25 in progress.

**27** Step 25 is completed. Open the bottom part.

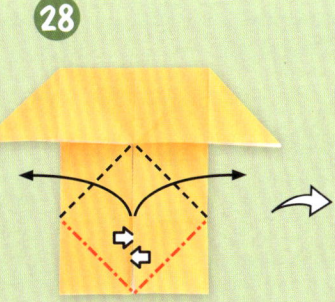
**28** Fold the bottom part in mirror image to step 25.

29
Step 28 is completed.

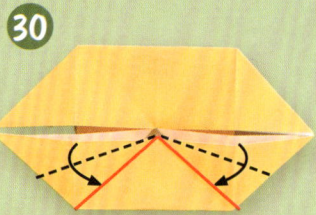
30
Fold the indicated edges to align with the creases.

31
Fold the flaps down again.

32
Fold both flaps corner to corner.

33
Step 32 is completed. Flip it over.

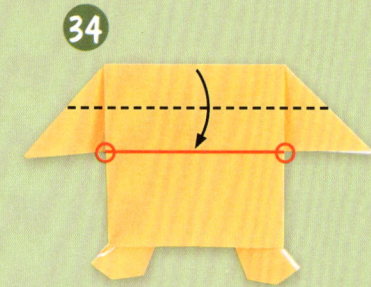
34
Fold the to edge down to align with the ○-to-○ span.

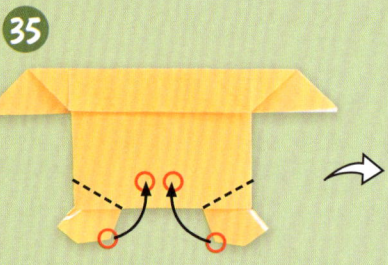
35
Fold so that the paired ○ points meet.

36
Fold along the spans between the paired ○ points.

37
Fold corner to corner so that the paired ○ points meet.

38
Fold so that the paired ○ points meet.

39
Fold small portions of both edges of the body to the back.

40
The Body is completed.

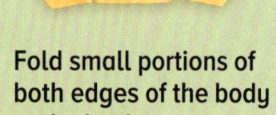
Completed

41
Insert the Body into the pocket in the Head and secure with a dab of glue to complete.

Try hanging the Rabbit's paws over a card for a cute presentation.

▶ Cute Pets

# Heart Hamster
▶ Photo on page 3

VIDEO:
tuttlepublishing.com/
unbelievably-cute-origami

You can fold me with a single sheet of paper—I'm even holding a heart!

Flat Version

Standing Version

- ▶ **Origami paper to use:** One 6-in (15-cm) sheet
- ▶ **Recommended tools:** Black felt tip pen, markers

## Standing Version

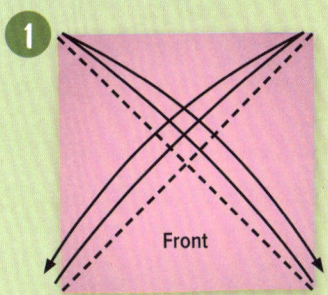

**1** Fold corner to corner both ways. Unfold after each. Flip it over.

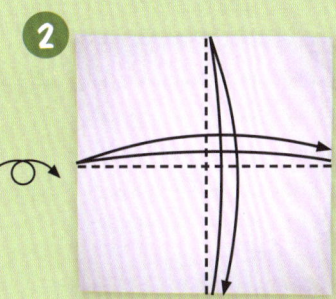

**2** Fold edge to edge both ways. Unfold after each.

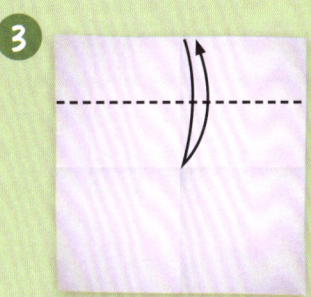

**3** Fold the top edge to meet the center crease. Unfold.

**4** Fold the top edge to the crease made in step 3.

**5** Step 4 is completed. Flip it over left to right.

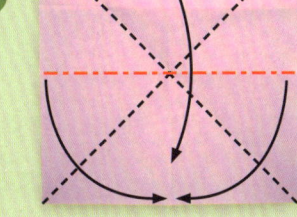

**6** Collapse the paper along the creases as shown in the Waterbomb Base instructions on page 15.

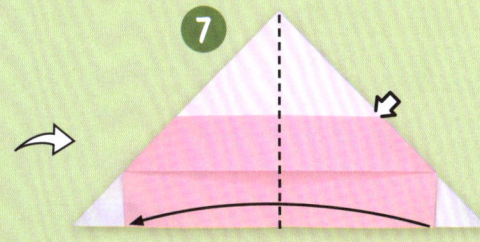

**7** Flip 1 layer to the left.

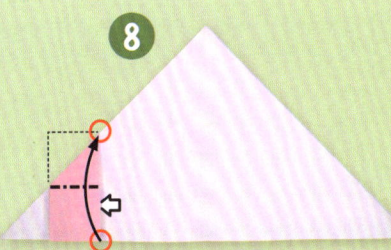

**8** Open the flap and pivot it while squashing so that the ○ points meet.

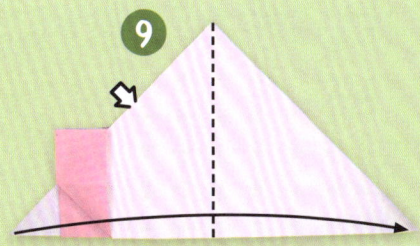

**9** Flip 2 layers to the right.

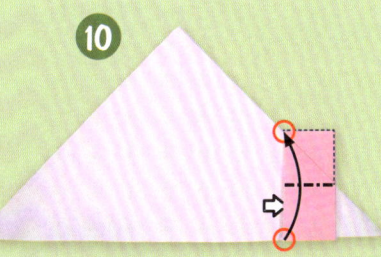

**10** Open the flap and pivot it while squashing so that the ○ points meet.

29

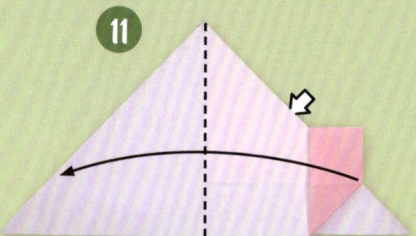

**11** Flip 1 layer to the left.

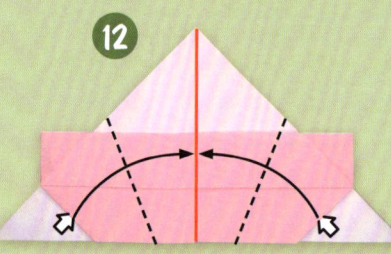

**12** Fold the edges in to align with the center.

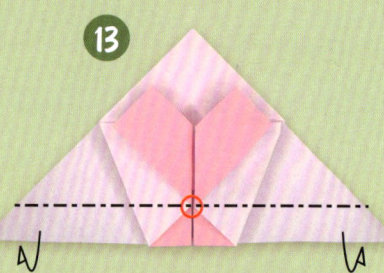

**13** Using the bottom point of the heart ○ as the landmark, fold a strip of the bottom edge to the back.

**14** Fold corner to corner on both sides. Unfold both. Flip it over.

**15** Inside reverse fold the corners along the creases from step 14.

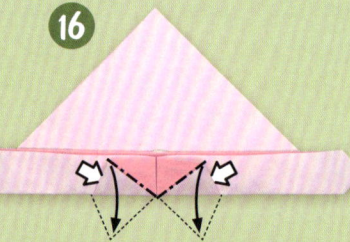

**16** Open slightly and collapse along the mountain folds.

**17** After collapsing. Flip to the other side.

**18** Fold along the spans between the paired ○ points.

**19** Open the flap slightly.

**20** Once opened, fold as shown in the diagram.

**21** Fold the corner as shown in the diagram.

**22** After folding, close the flap.

**23** After closing. Fold the left side in mirror image to steps 19–22.

**24** Step 23 is completed. Flip it over.

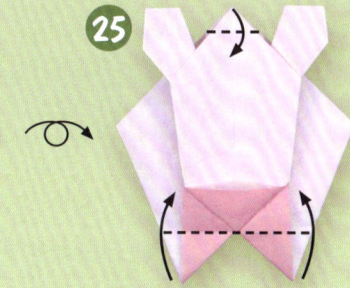

**25** Fold down a small portion of the top corner, and fold up the bottom corners along the existing creases.

**26** Fold in 4 locations as indicated.

Approx. 3/8 in (1 cm)

**27** Step 26 is completed. Flip it over.

**28** Make mountain folds on the top heart corners and valley folds on the side heart corners.

**29** Draw the face and color in the coat markings. Flip it over.

**30** Open the triangular flaps downward.

**Flat Version**

**31** Open both sides to form 3D shapes.

**32** Adjust the shapes to make it stand upright.

**Completed**

**33** The Standing Version is completed.

**30** Begin from the state at the start of step 30. Fold the bottom corners diagonally downward.

**31** Flip it over.

**Completed**

**32** The Flat Version is completed.

31

▶ LIVELY ZOO ANIMALS

# Lion
▶ Photo on page 4

VIDEO:
tuttlepublishing.com/
unbelievably-cute-origami

I'm made with three sheets of paper. My majestic mane is impressive!

- **Origami paper to use:** Mane: One 6-in (15-cm) sheet / Face: One 3-in (7.5-cm) sheet / Body: One 6-in (15-cm) sheet
- **Recommended tools:** Black felt tip pen, markers, glue or masking tape

## Mane

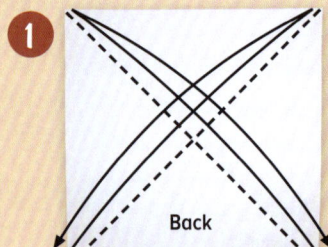

**1** Fold corner to corner both ways. Unfold after each.

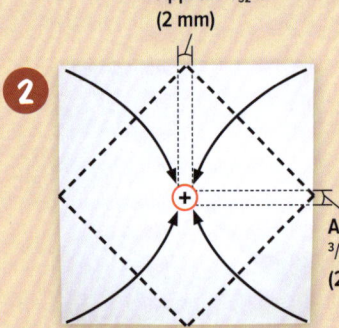

**2** Fold the corners in to points just short of the center so that the adjacent edges have 3/32-in (2-mm) gaps (approx.) between them.

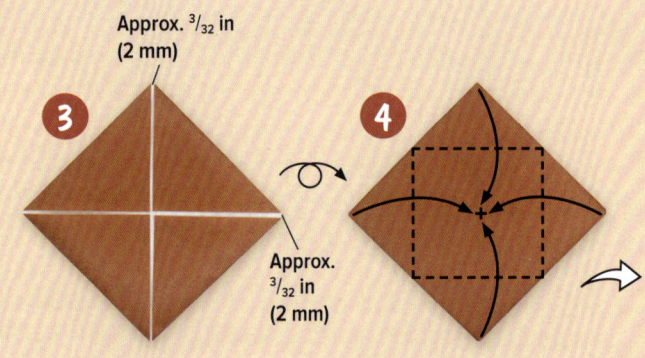

**3** Here, the 3/32-in (2-mm) gaps are visible. Flip it over.

**4** Fold each corner to the center.

**5** Step 4 is completed. Flip it over.

**6** Fold in the corners as indicated.

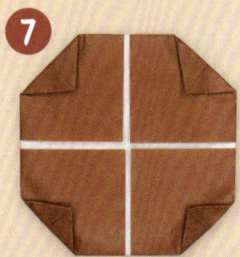

**7** Step 6 is completed. Flip it over.

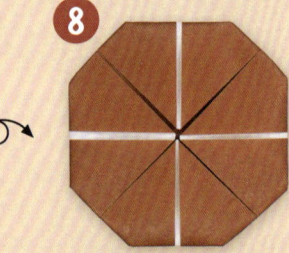

**8** The Mane is completed.

## Face

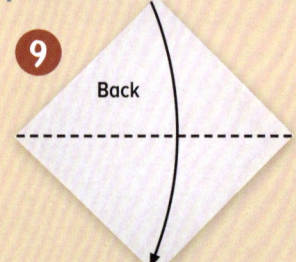

**9** Fold the paper in half corner to corner.

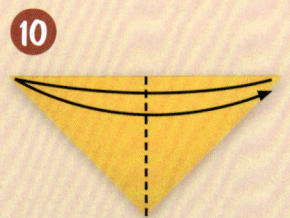

**10** Fold corner to corner. Unfold.

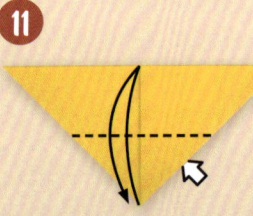

**11** Fold the bottom corner of the uppermost flap to the top edge. Unfold.

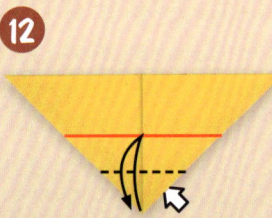

**12** Fold the bottom corner of the uppermost flap to the crease from step 11. Unfold.

**13**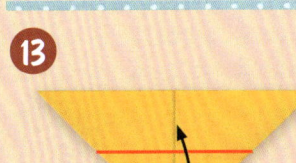
Fold up the uppermost flap to bring the step 11 and step 12 creases together.

**14**
Fold the corner of the uppermost flap to meet the step-12 crease. Unfold.

**15**
Fold the corner of the uppermost flap to meet the step-14 crease.

**16**
Refold along the step-14 crease.

**17**
Step 16 is completed. Flip it over.

**18**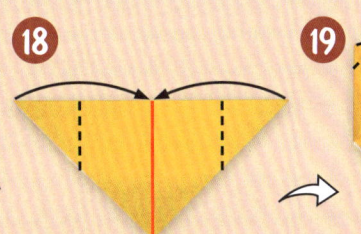
Fold the corners to the center.

**19**
Fold in small portions of the corners.

**20**
Fold the diagonal edges out to meet the left and right vertical edges.

**21**
Fold corner to corner on both sides.

**22**
Step 21 is completed. Flip it over.

**23**
The Face is completed.

**24**
Insert the Face into the Mane.

**25**
Draw on the face. The Head is completed.

## Body

**26**
Begin with a Waterbomb Base (page 15) with the fur color on the outside.

**27**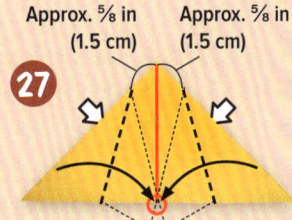
Approx. ⅝ in (1.5 cm)   Approx. ⅝ in (1.5 cm)
From ⅝ in (1.5 cm) below the top, fold the side edges to pass through the center.

**28**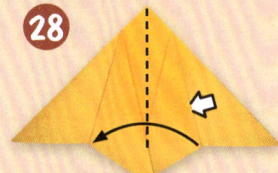
Flip 1 layer to the left.

**29**
Fold the uppermost layer to the right, bringing the corner to the center.

**30**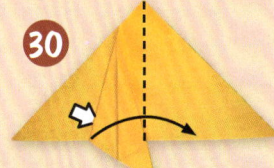
Flip 2 layers to the right.

**31**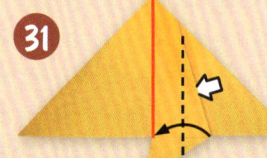
Fold the uppermost layer to the left, bringing the corner to the center.

**32**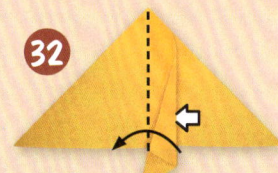
Flip 1 layer to the left.

**33**
Step 32 is completed. Flip it over.

33

**34** Fold the left edge to the center. Unfold.

**35** Starting from the ○ point at the bottom of the step-34 crease, fold the corner to the edge.

**36** Fold in along the existing crease.

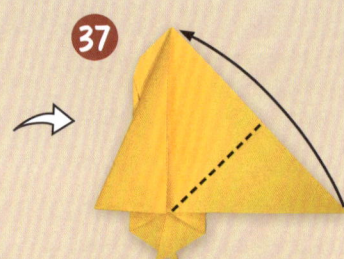
**37** Fold corner to corner.

**38** Fold the corner to the center.

**39** Unfold the flap marked ※ to return it to its step-37 state.

**40** Step 39 is completed.

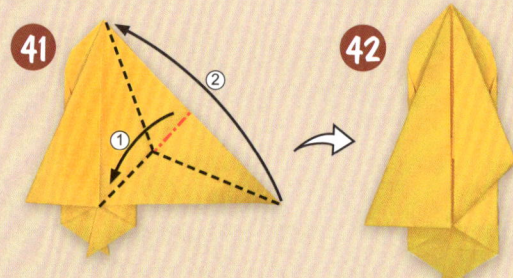
**41** Fold in the order of ①, then ②.

**42** Step 42 is completed.

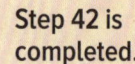

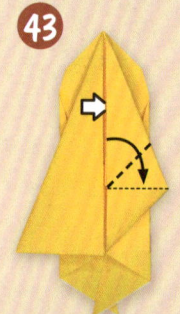
**43** Fold the flap as indicated.

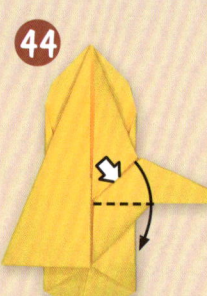
**44** Flip the flap down along the existing crease.

**45** Fold the flap up to align with the diagonal edge.

**46** Flip 1 layer to the left.

**47** Fold as indicated.

**48** Enlarged view.

**49** Tuck the flap marked ※ inside the underlying pocket.

**50** Step 49 is completed. Flip it over.

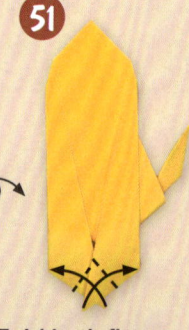
**51** Fold both flaps corner to corner.

**52** Fold the paws to stand perpendicular to the Body.

**53** The Body is completed.

**54** **Completed**
Attach the Head. The Lion is completed!

▶ LIVELY ZOO ANIMALS

# Elephant
▶ Photo on page 4

VIDEO:
tuttlepublishing.com/
unbelievably-cute-origami

I'm folded from one sheet of paper. I'm big, and my wide ears make me charming.

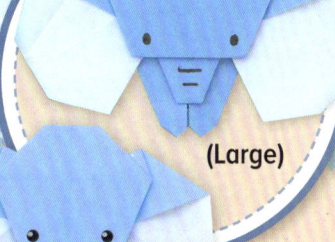
(Large)

(Small)

▸ **Origami paper to use:** Large: One 6⅞-in (17.5-cm) sheet / Small: One 6-in (15-cm) sheet
▸ **Recommended tools:** Black felt tip pen, round stickers (black, ³⁄₁₆ in / 5 mm)

➔ The following instructions show 6-in (15-cm) origami paper being used.

❶

Start with a Square Base (page 14) with the hide color on the outside, open side at the bottom.

❷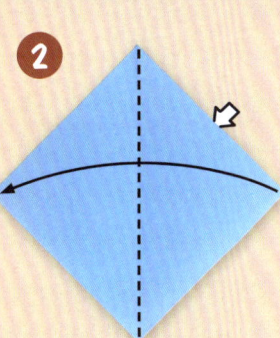

Flip 1 layer to the left.

❸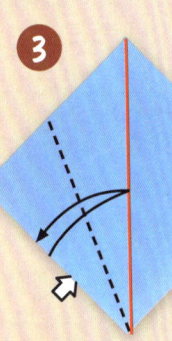

Fold the edge of the uppermost flap to the center. Unfold.

❹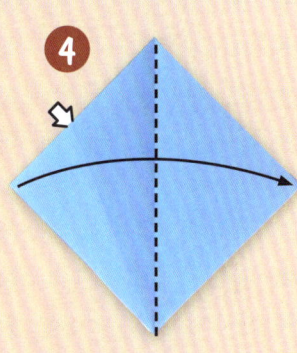

Flip 1 layer to the right.

❺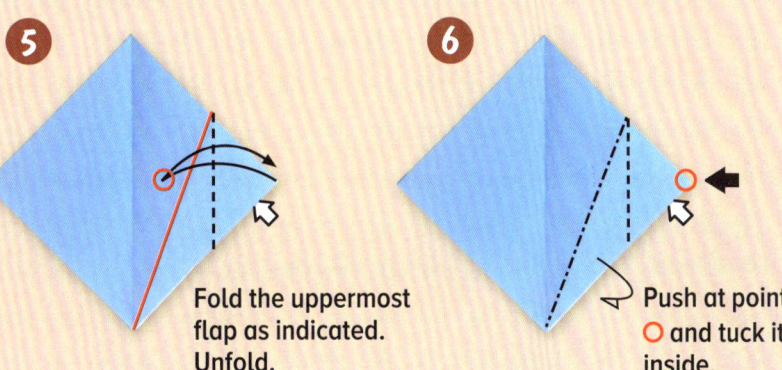

Fold the uppermost flap as indicated. Unfold.

❻ 

Push at point ○ and tuck it inside.

❼

Step 6 in progress.

❽

Step 6 is completed.

❾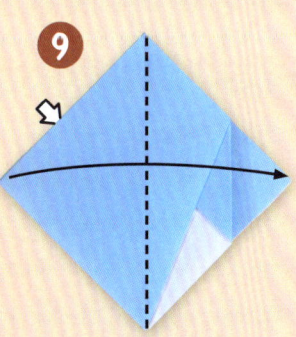

Fold the left side in mirror image to steps 2–6.

❿

Step 9 is completed. Flip it over left to right.

⓫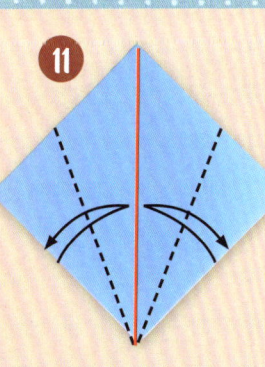

Fold the edges to the center. Unfold both.

35

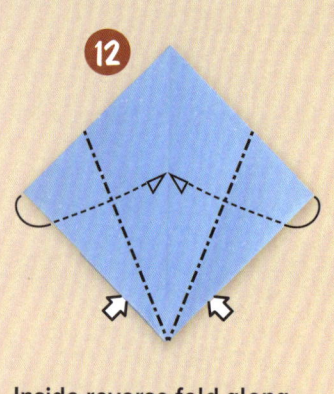

12 Inside reverse fold along the creases from step 11.

13 Step 12 in progress.

14 Step 12 is completed.

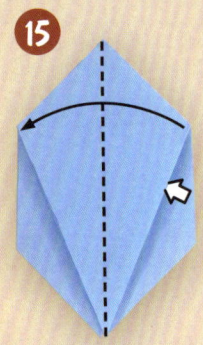

15 Flip 1 layer to the left.

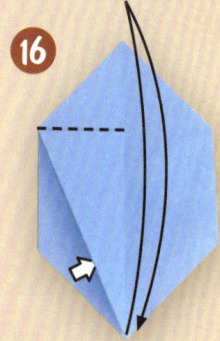

16 Open from the bottom and crease only the left side.

17 Crease only in the location.

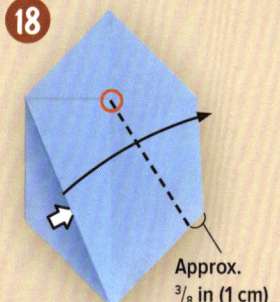

18 Fold from about 3/8 in (1 cm) down from the corner to the intersection of creases ○.

Approx. 3/8 in (1 cm)

19 Step 18 in progress. Squash the pocket that forms at the top as you fold.

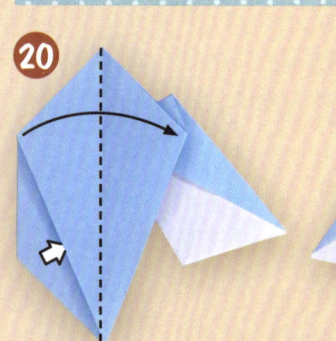

20 Step 19 is completed. Mirror steps 15–19 on the left side.

21 Step 20 is completed.

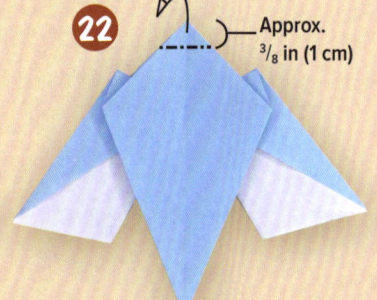

22 Fold a small portion of the top corner to the back.

Approx. 3/8 in (1 cm)

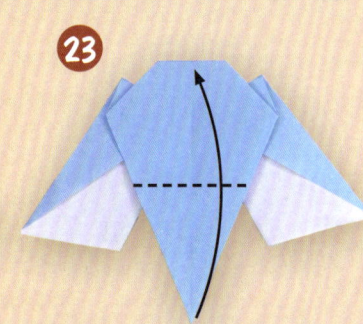

23 Fold the uppermost flap of the bottom corner up to the center of the top edge.

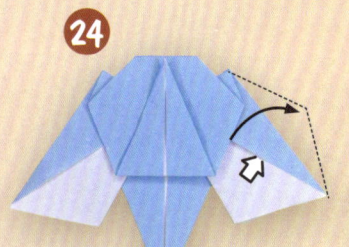

24 Open slightly and pull to the right while shifting the paper. Squash it flat.

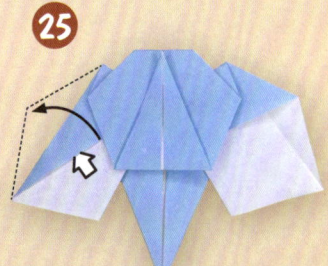

25 Fold the left side in mirror image to step 24.

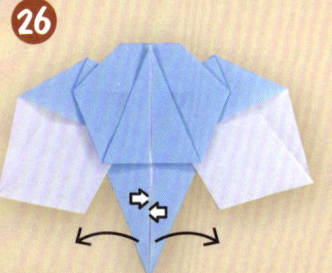

26 Open up the bottom flap from the middle.

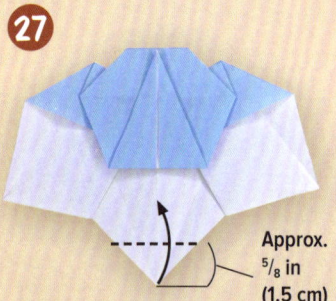

27 Fold up the bottom corner.

Approx. 5/8 in (1.5 cm)

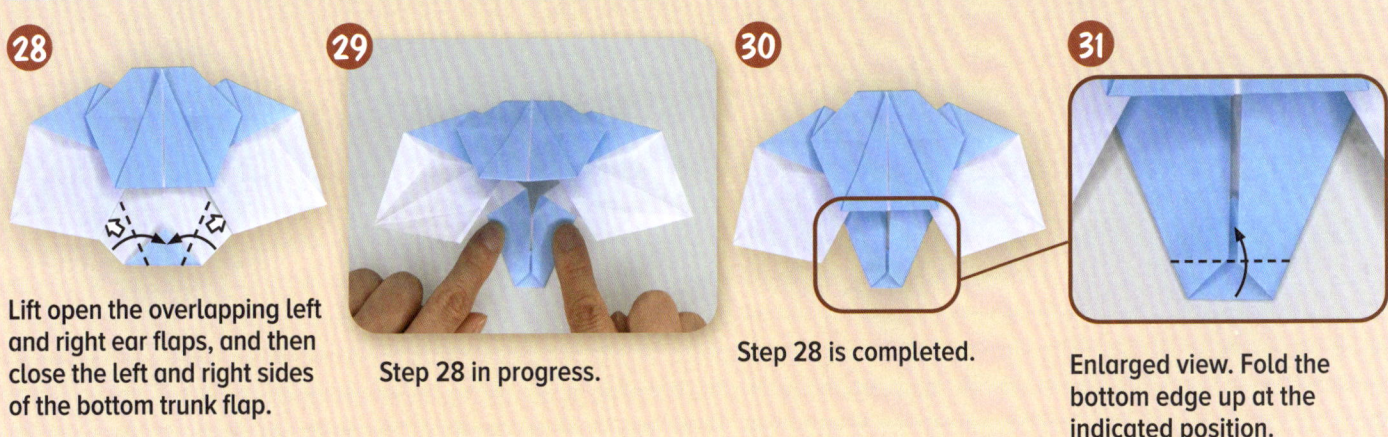

**28** Lift open the overlapping left and right ear flaps, and then close the left and right sides of the bottom trunk flap.

**29** Step 28 in progress.

**30** Step 28 is completed.

**31** Enlarged view. Fold the bottom edge up at the indicated position.

 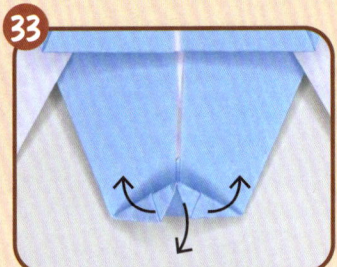 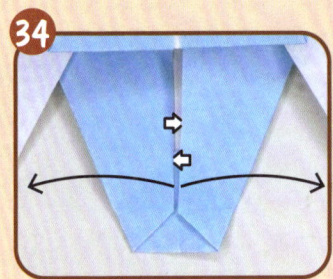 

**32** Fold down the corners at the indicated positions.

**33** Step 32 is completed. Return the flap to the state at the beginning of step 31.

**34** Open to the left and right.

**35** Fold up along the existing horizontal crease.

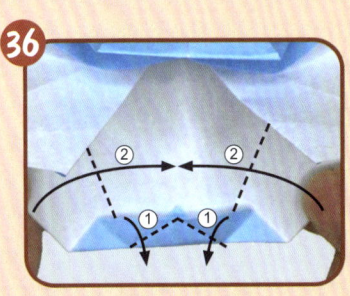  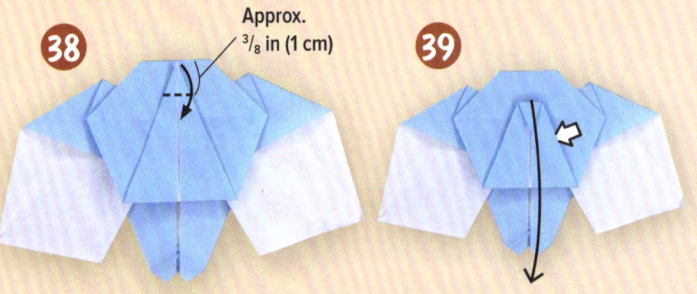

**36** Fold in order: ①, then ② to close the sides.

**37** Step 36 is completed.

**38** Fold down the top corner of the trunk flap. Approx. 3/8 in (1 cm)

**39** Swing the flap down on the existing crease.

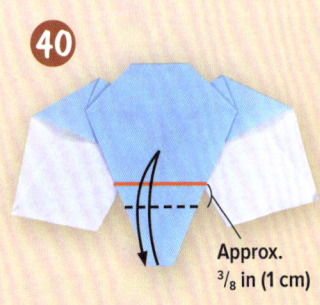 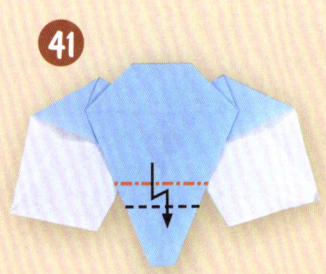  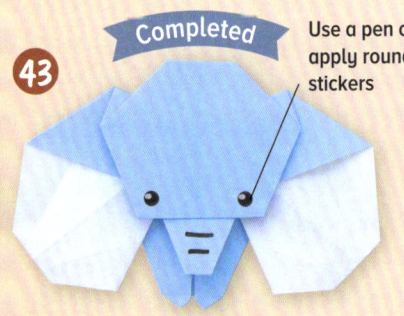

**40** Make a crease about 3/8 in (1 cm) below the fold crease step 39.

**41** Reverse the crease used in step 39 to make it a mountain fold, and a valley fold along the crease from step 40.

**42** Fold the lower left and right corners to the back.

**43** **Completed** Use a pen or apply round stickers. Draw on the face to complete the Elephant.

▶ LIVELY ZOO ANIMALS

# Gorilla
▶ Photo on page 5

VIDEO:
tuttlepublishing.com/
unbelievably-cute-origami

I'm made from two sheets of paper. My rice-ball-shaped head is comical.

- **Origami paper to use:** Head: One 3-in (7.5-cm) sheet / Body: One 6-in (15-cm) sheet
- **Recommended tools:** Black felt tip pen, glue or masking tape

## Head

**1**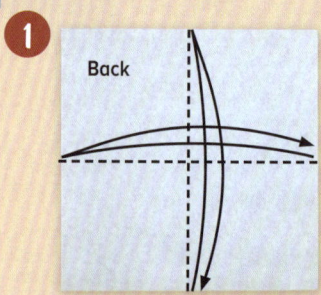
Fold edge to edge both ways. Unfold after each.

**2**
Fold the top corners to the center. Unfold both. Flip it over.

**3**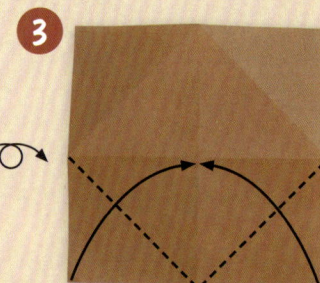
Fold the bottom corners to the center.

**4**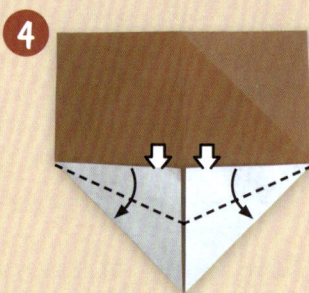
Bisect the angles by folding the horizontal flap edges to meet the diagonal outside edges.

**5**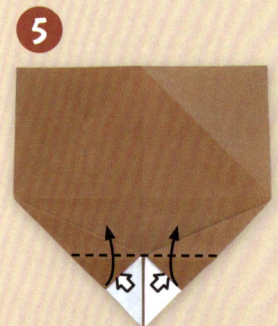
Fold the 2 flap corners up at the indicated positions.

**6**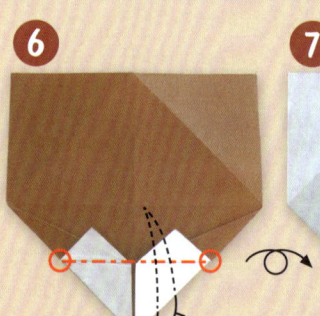
Mountain fold along the ○-to-○ span. Unfold. Flip it over.

**7**
Fold the bottom corner to the crease made in step 6.

**8**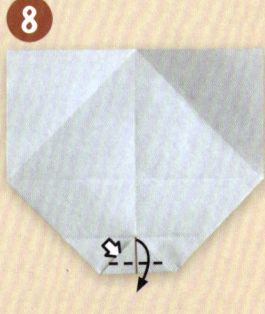
Fold a portion of the flap down so that the tip protrudes to the bottom.

**9**
Fold along the existing crease.

**10**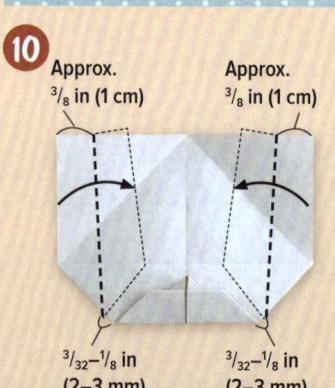
Approx. ³⁄₈ in (1 cm)   Approx. ³⁄₈ in (1 cm)
³⁄₃₂–¹⁄₈ in (2–3 mm)   ³⁄₃₂–¹⁄₈ in (2–3 mm)
Fold at the indicated positions.

**11**
Fold the top corners to the center.

**12**
Tuck the excess part (※) inside.

**13**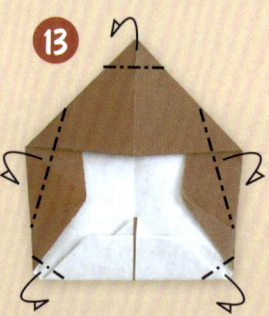
Mountain fold 5 corners to the back.

**14**
Draw on the face to complete the Head.

# Body

**15**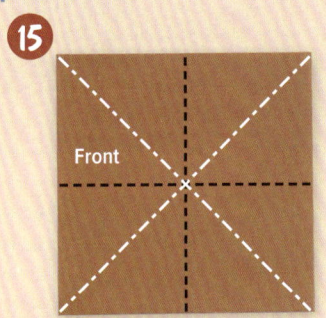
Make creases as shown in the diagram.

**16**
Fold the corner to the center.

**17**
Flip it over.

**18**
Collapse the paper like a Waterbomb Base (page 15).

**19**
Fold the edge to the center. Unfold.

**20**
Open the flap and squash it into a diamond shape.

**21**
Fold the corners to meet at a point along the central axis.

**22** Approx. ¾ in (2 cm)
Fold the corners to the back.

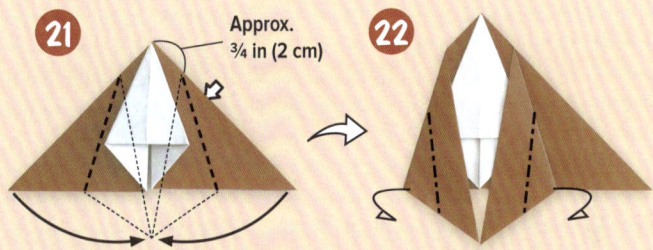

**23** Flip it over.

**24** Fold corner to corner on both flaps.

**25** Enlarged view.

**26** Fold up small portions of the corners.

**27** Step 26 is completed.

**28** Flip 1 layer to the right.

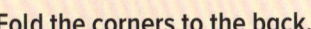

**29** Approx. ⅜ in (1 cm)
Fold at the indicated position.

**30** Flip it over.

**31** Fold as indicated, starting on the right.

**32** Fold the right corner to the back.

**33** The Body is completed.

**34** Completed
Attach the Head to complete.

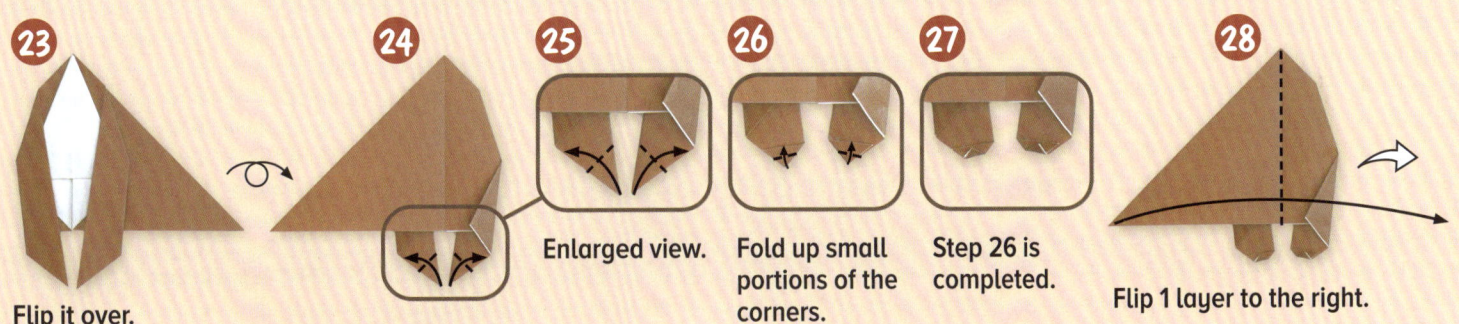
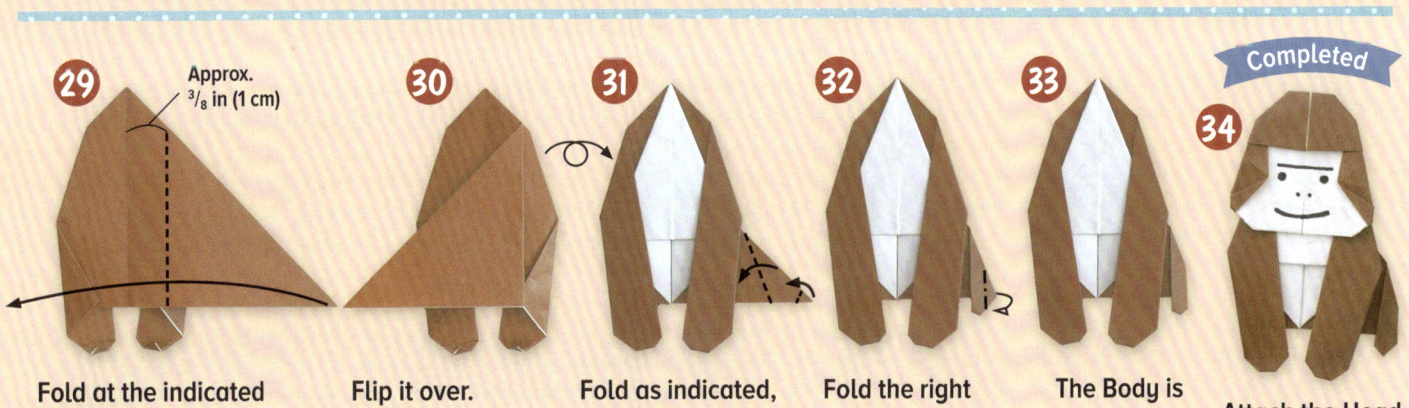

39

# ► LIVELY ZOO ANIMALS

# Panda
► Photo on page 5

VIDEO: tuttlepublishing.com/unbelievably-cute-origami

I was cleverly designed so that the colored areas appear on the eyes, nose, ears and paws!

Large

Small

- ► **Origami paper to use:**
  Head (Large): One 6-in (15-cm) sheet / Body (Large): One 6-in (15-cm) sheet;
  Head (Small): One 4-in (10-cm) sheet / Body (Small): One 4-in (10-cm) sheet
- ► **Recommended tools:** Black felt tip pen, round stickers (for Large: white, 5/8 in / 1.5 cm, black, 5/16 in / 8 mm; for Small: white, 5/16 in / 8 mm; black, 3/16 in / 5 mm), glue or masking tape
- → The following instructions show 6-in (15-cm) origami paper being used.

## Head

**1**
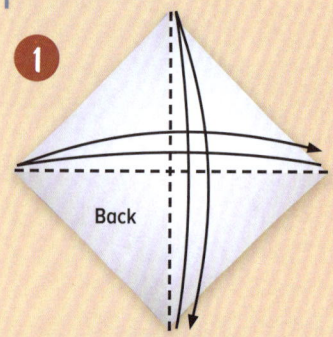
Fold corner to corner both ways. Unfold after each.

**2**

Fold the corner to the center.

**3**

Fold the corner to the edge.

**4**
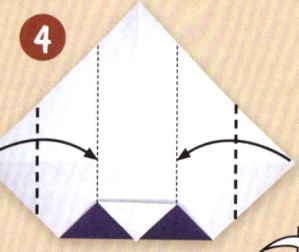
Fold the side corners to the indicated positions.

**5**

Fold the top half behind along the existing crease.

**6**

Fold the bottom corner to meet the indicated edge.

**7**

Fold down a small portion of the flap.

**8**

Fold in small strips along the diagonal edges.

**9**

Unfold the top layer of both strips folded in step 8.

**10**

Reverse the creases at the edges of the remaining folded strips (※), and tuck them inside.

**11**

Refold the strips that were unfolded in step 9.

**12**

Fold the top corners behind at the indicated locations.

Step 12 is completed. Flip it over.

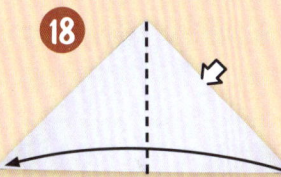
Fold out the triangular flaps at the marked position.

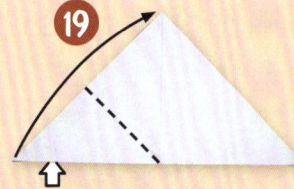
Flip it over again.

Apply round eye stickers and draw on the mouth. The Head is completed.

## Body

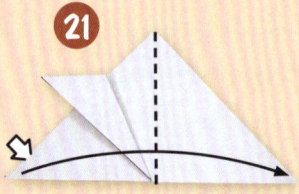
Start with a Waterbomb Base (page 15) with the main fur color on the outside.

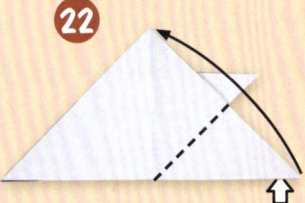
Flip 1 layer to the left.

Fold the uppermost layer corner to corner.

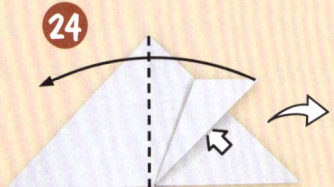
Fold the vertical edge to meet the diagonal edge.

Flip 2 layers to the right.

Fold the uppermost layer corner to corner.

Fold the vertical edge to meet the diagonal edge.

Flip 1 layer to the left.

Fold so that the paired ○ points meet.

Unfold the paper completely.

Step 26 is completed.

Fold along the indicated lines to form mountain folds.

Step 28 in progress. Flip it over.

Fold the bottom corners to meet the adjacent crease intersections.

Begin collapsing along the creases.

41

**32** The bottom corners have been folded.

**33** Fold the top corners and collapse the model.

**34** The model collapse is completed. Flip it over.

**35** Mountain fold the left and right triangular flaps to the inside.

**36** Step 35 is completed. Flip it over.

**37** Fold up both layers of a ³⁄₈–⁵⁄₈-in (1–1.5-cm) strip at the bottom. Approx. ³⁄₈–⁵⁄₈ in (1–1.5 cm)

**38** Open 1 layer.

**39** Tuck the opened flap inside.

**40** Tuck in the part marked ※ with a mountain fold.

**41** Fold down the arm flaps as indicated.

**42** The Body is completed.

**43** *Completed*
Attach the Head to complete.

### Tips for Drawing Faces & Markings

**① Using pens (black or colored)**

 Ⓐ
 Ⓑ
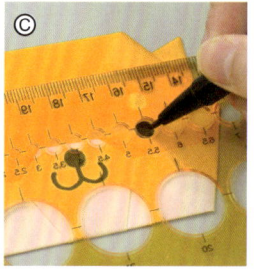 Ⓒ

Ⓐ Refer to the finished example photos and draw the eyes, nose, etc. with a felt tip pen.
Ⓑ Use markers to decorate the bodies freely with adorable features.
Ⓒ Use a circle template ruler for neatly filled-in circles.

**② Using round stickers**

 Ⓐ
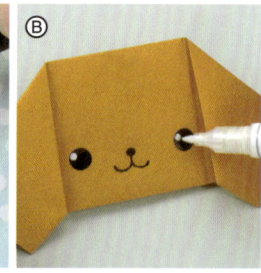 Ⓑ

Ⓐ Use the provided round stickers (or use your own) to make the eyes. You can also color in the eyes using a felt tip pen.
Ⓑ For extra cuteness, add sparkles to solid black pupils using a white paint pen.

▶ LIVELY ZOO ANIMALS

# Tiger
▶ Photo on page 4

VIDEO:
tuttlepublishing.com/
unbelievably-cute-origami

The white tufts around my cheeks are a key detail. My features are drawn in with a felt tip pen.

Large

Small

- **Origami paper to use:** Head (Large): One 6-in (15-cm) sheet / Body (Large): One 6-in (15-cm) sheet; Head (Small): One 4¾-in (12-cm) sheet / Body (Small): One 4¾-in (12-cm) sheet
- **Recommended tools:** Black felt tip pen, markers, glue or masking tape

→ The following instructions show 6-in (15-cm) origami paper being used.

**Head**

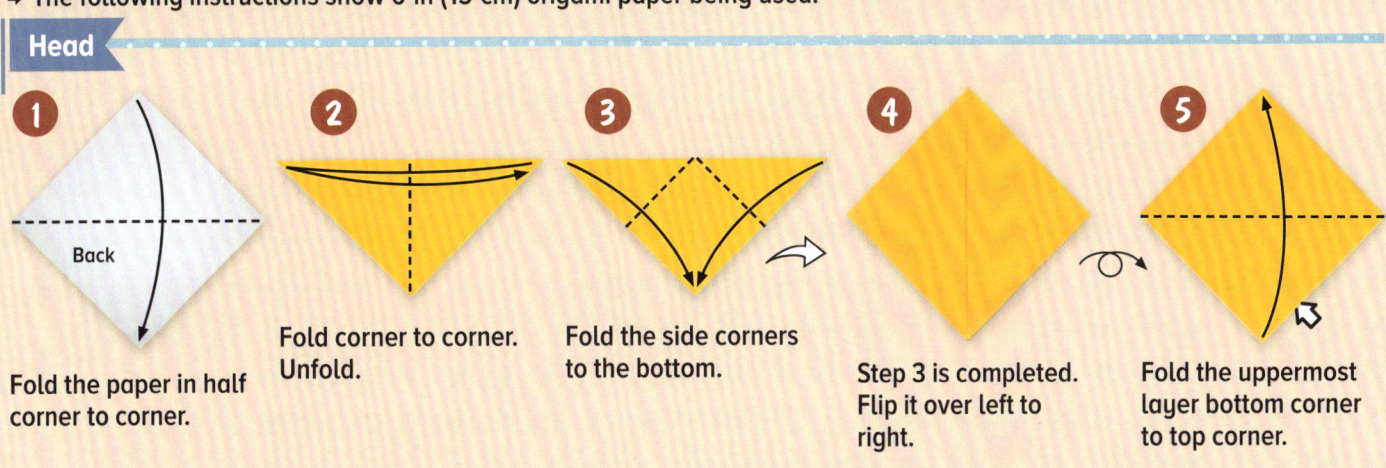

**1** Fold the paper in half corner to corner.

**2** Fold corner to corner. Unfold.

**3** Fold the side corners to the bottom.

**4** Step 3 is completed. Flip it over left to right.

**5** Fold the uppermost layer bottom corner to top corner.

**6** Fold the uppermost layer of the top corner to the center. Unfold.

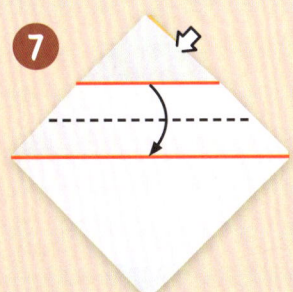
**7** Fold so that the crease made in step 6 meets the center horizontal crease.

**8** Fold the corner to meet the edge formed in step 7.

**9** Fold down a small portion of the flap.

**10** Flip it over left to right.

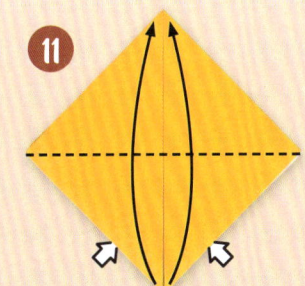
**11** Fold the flaps to the top.

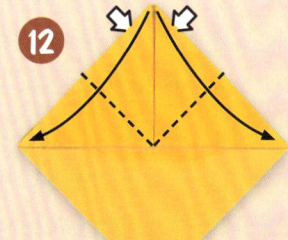
**12** Fold the top corners of the uppermost flaps to meet the respective side corners.

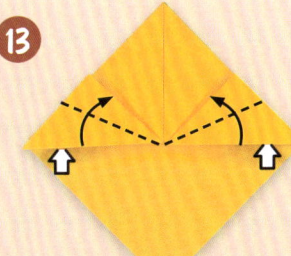
**13** Fold the flaps up edge to edge.

43

**14** Fold in small portions of all 4 corners.

**15** Fold down a small portion of the top corner, and fold the bottom corner to the center.

**16** Fold so that the 2 ○ points at the bottom meet in the center.

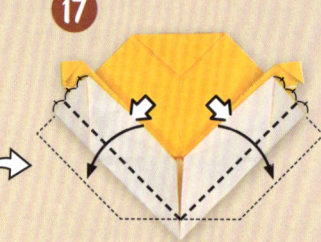
**17** Fold portions of the step-16 flaps back out as indicated.

**18** Fold so that ○ and ○ line up.

**19** Tuck the overlapping step-18 flap inside.

**20** Step 19 is completed. Flip it over.

**21** Draw on the face and color in the coat markings. The Head is completed.

## Body

**22** Start with a Waterbomb Base (page 15) with the fur color on the outside.

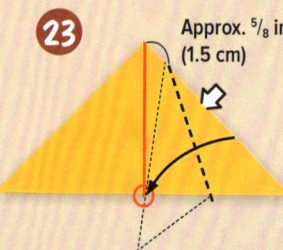
**23** Fold with the crease starting ⅝ in (1.5 cm) from the top corner, with long edge passing through the center of the bottom edge.

**24** Fold the left side in mirror image to the flap from step 23.

**25** Step 24 is completed. Flip it over.

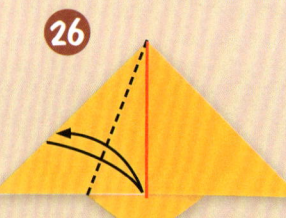
**26** Fold the edge to the center. Unfold.

**27** Fold the bottom edge up to align with the step-26 crease.

**28** Refold along the step-26 crease.

**29** Flip 1 layer to the right.

**30** Fold the corner to the central vertical crease.

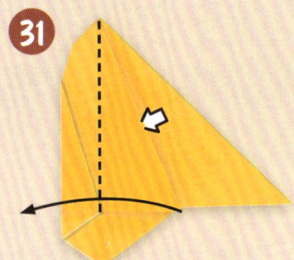
**31** Flip the layer back to the left.

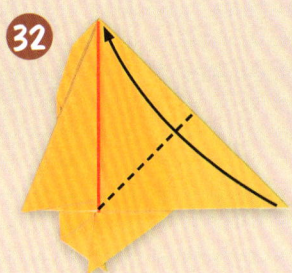
**32** Fold corner to corner.

**33** Fold the edge to the center. Unfold. Return the flap to the state at the beginning of step 32.

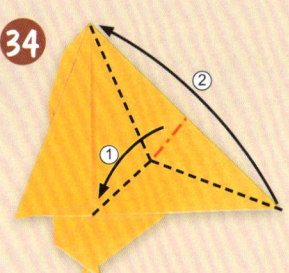
**34** Collapse the precreased flap in the order of steps ①, then ②.

**35** Step 34 is completed.

**36** Fold the flap as shown. Unfold.

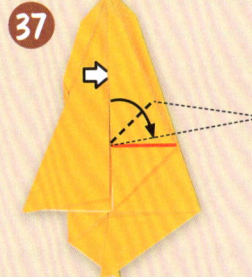
**37** Fold from the left end of the step-36 crease, giving the flap a small angle of elevation.

**38** Fold down along the existing crease.

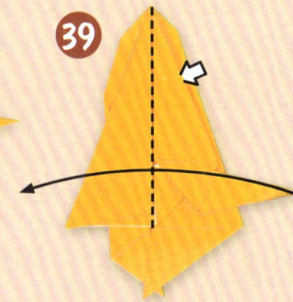
**39** Flip 1 layer to the left.

**40** Open the flap and tuck the small tab indicated with the ↗ into the pocket marked with ✕.

**41** Step 40 in progress.

**42** Fold the corner to the center.

**43** Step 42 is completed. Flip it over.

**44** Fold both flaps corner to corner.

**45** Enlarged view of step 44.

**46** Fold the paws to stand perpendicular to the Body.

**47** Step 46 is completed.

**48** Color in the coat markings. The Body is completed.

**49** Completed
Insert the Body into the Head pocket and secure with glue to complete.

▶ LIVELY ZOO ANIMALS

# Tree, Leaves & Grass
▶ Photo on page 4

VIDEO: tuttlepublishing.com/unbelievably-cute-origami

If folded from warmer colors, these can also be used to depict autumn foliage.

Tree  Leaf  Grass

- **Origami paper to use:** Tree Top (Large): One 4-in (10-cm) sheet / Tree Trunk (Large): One 4-in (10-cm) sheet; Tree Top (Small): One 3-in (7.5-cm) sheet / Tree Trunk (Small): One 3-in (7.5-cm) sheet; Leaf: One 1$^{3}/_{16}$-in (3-cm) sheet; Grass: One 2-in (5-cm) sheet
- **Recommended tool:** Glue

➡ The following instructions show 3-in (7.5-cm) origami paper being used.

## Tree Top

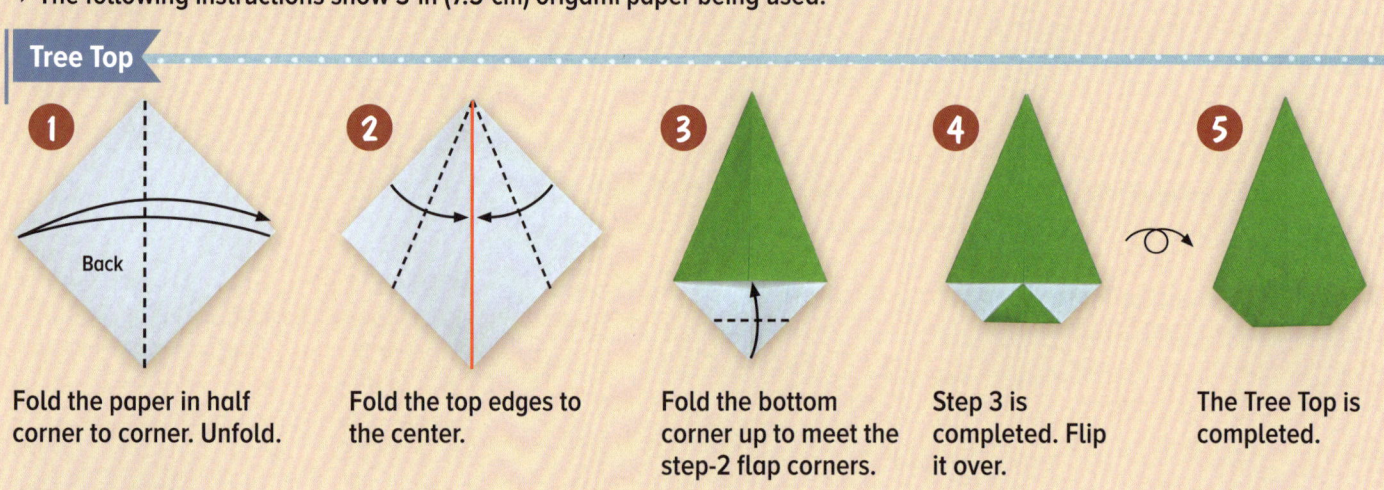

**1** Fold the paper in half corner to corner. Unfold.

**2** Fold the top edges to the center.

**3** Fold the bottom corner up to meet the step-2 flap corners.

**4** Step 3 is completed. Flip it over.

**5** The Tree Top is completed.

## Tree Trunk

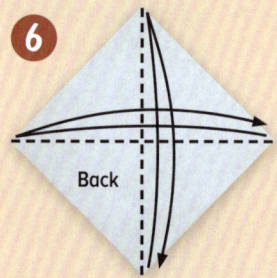
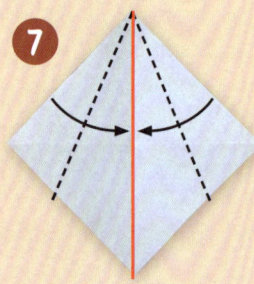

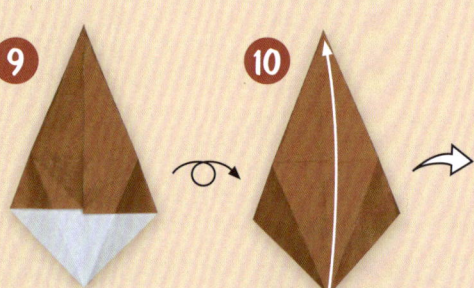

**6** Fold corner to corner both ways. Unfold after each.

**7** Fold the top edges to the center.

**8** Fold the bottom edges to the center. Unfold both.

**9** Step 8 is completed. Flip it over.

**10** Bring the bottom corner to the top, but don't make a crease.

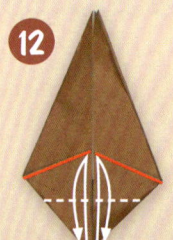
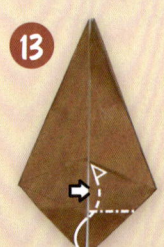
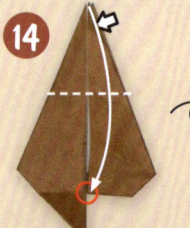
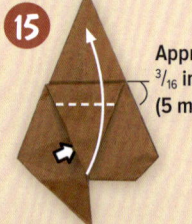

**11** Open the pockets and collapse them along the existing creases.

**12** Fold the flaps to the point where the creases converge. Unfold both.

**13** Inside reverse fold only on the right side.

**14** Fold down the uppermost layer, aligning the tip with the ○.

**15** Fold up the corner at the indicated position. Approx. $^{3}/_{16}$ in (5 mm)

**16** Fold in half.

**17** Pull out the hidden flap and squash it.

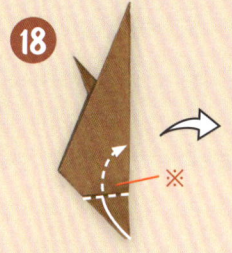
**18** Insert the bottom corner into the ※ pocket.

**19** Step 18 in progress.

**20** Step 18 is completed. Flip it over.

**21** The Tree Trunk is completed. Attach it to the Tree Top from step 5.

**22** Completed
The Tree is completed.

➡ The following instructions show 1 3/16-in (3-cm) origami paper being used.

## Leaf

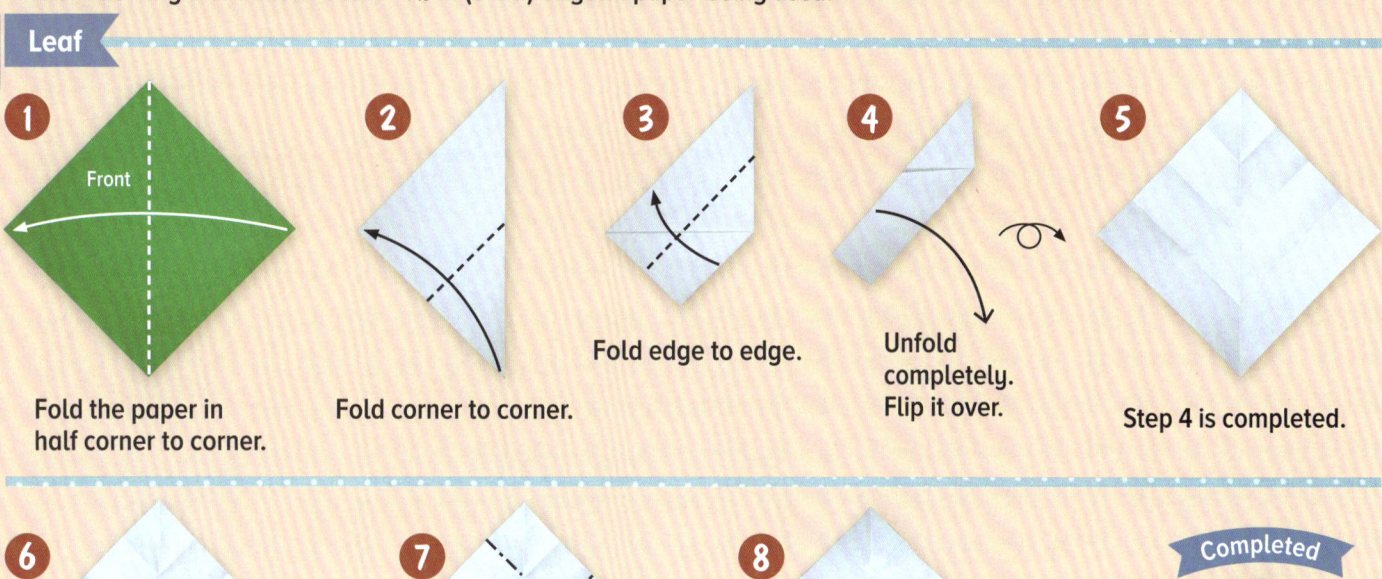

**1** Fold the paper in half corner to corner.
**2** Fold corner to corner.
**3** Fold edge to edge.
**4** Unfold completely. Flip it over.
**5** Step 4 is completed.

**6** Fold the edges to align with the creases.
**7** Change the indicated existing valley creases into mountain creases.
**8** Step 7 is completed. Flip it over.
**9** Completed
The Leaf is completed.

➡ The following instructions show 2-in (5-cm) origami paper being used.

## Grass

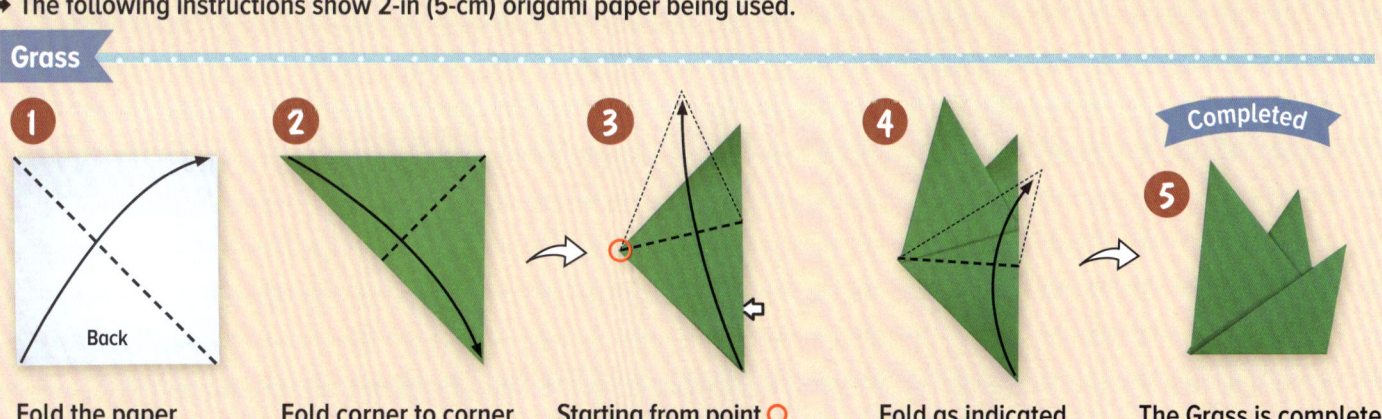

**1** Fold the paper in half corner to corner.
**2** Fold corner to corner.
**3** Starting from point ○, fold the uppermost layer of the bottom corner as indicated.
**4** Fold as indicated.
**5** Completed
The Grass is completed.

## FRIENDLY FOREST ANIMALS

# Fox
▶ Photo on page 6

VIDEO:
tuttlepublishing.com/
unbelievably-cute-origami

If you make large and small versions using 6-in (15-cm) and 4¾-in (12-cm) sheets, you can display us like a parent and kit!

Small   Large

- **Origami paper to use:** Head (Large): One 6-in (15-cm) sheet / Body (Large): One 6-in (15-cm) sheet; Head (Small): One 4¾-in (12-cm) sheet / Body (Small): One 4¾-in (12-cm) sheet
- **Recommended tools:** Black felt tip pen, markers, white paint pen, round stickers (for Large: white, ⅝ in / 1.5 cm; for Small: white, 5⁄16 in / 8 mm), glue or masking tape
➜ The following instructions show 6-in (15-cm) origami paper being used.

### Head

**1** Fold the paper in half corner to corner.

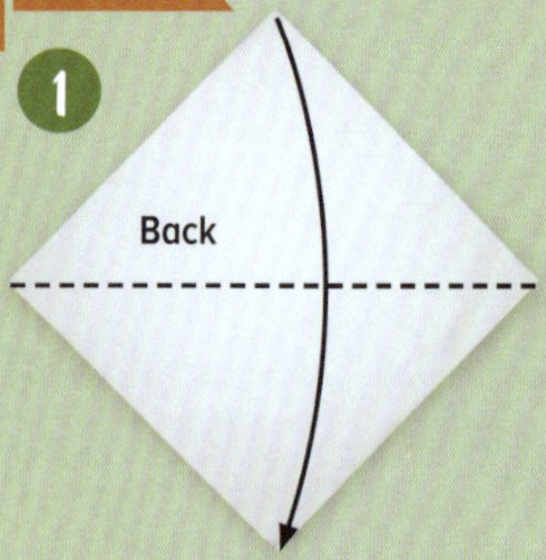

**2** Fold corner to corner. Unfold.

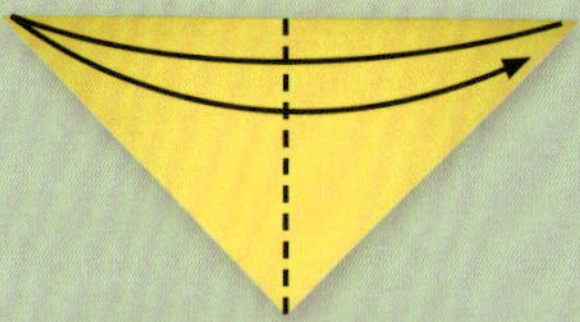

**3** Fold both layers of the bottom corner to meet the top edge. Unfold.

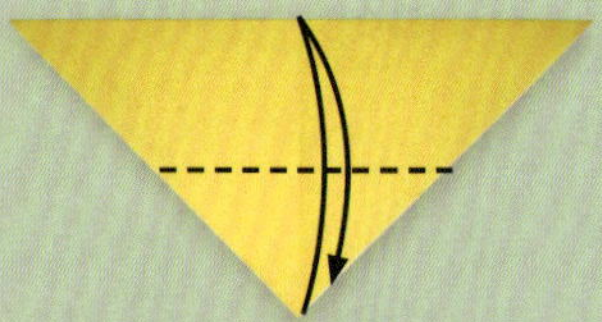

**4** Fold the side corners to the bottom.

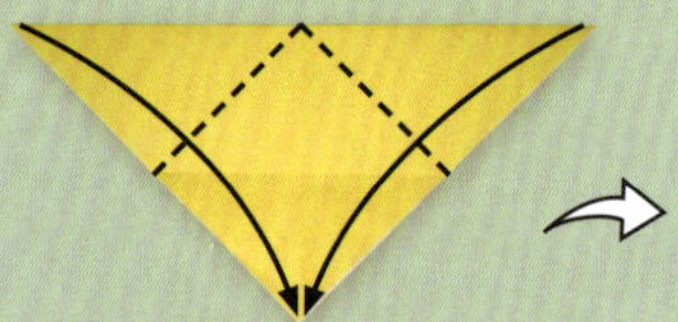

**5** Fold the flaps up diagonally as indicated. (Approx. 1 in (2.5 cm); Approx. ⅜ in (1 cm))

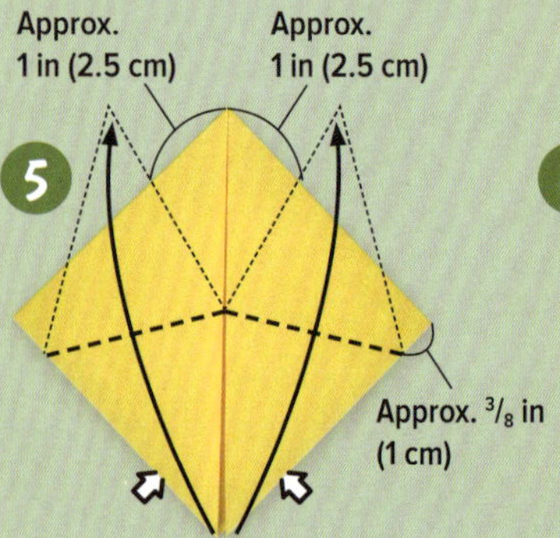

**6** Open the flaps slightly and pivot to shift the layers as indicated, then squash. (Approx. ⅜ in (1 cm))

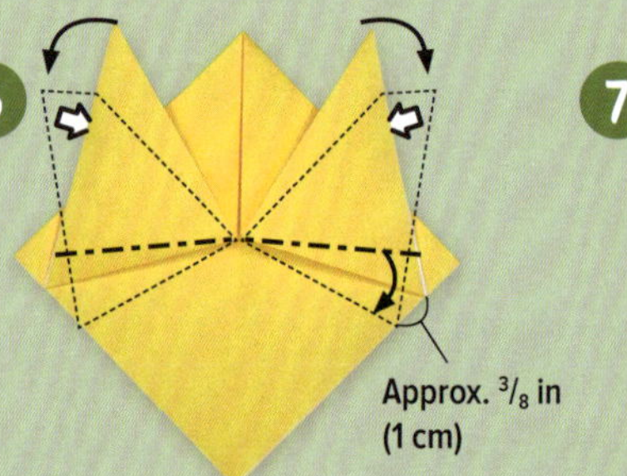

**7** Fold the corner down as indicated. (Approx. ⅝ in (1.5 cm))

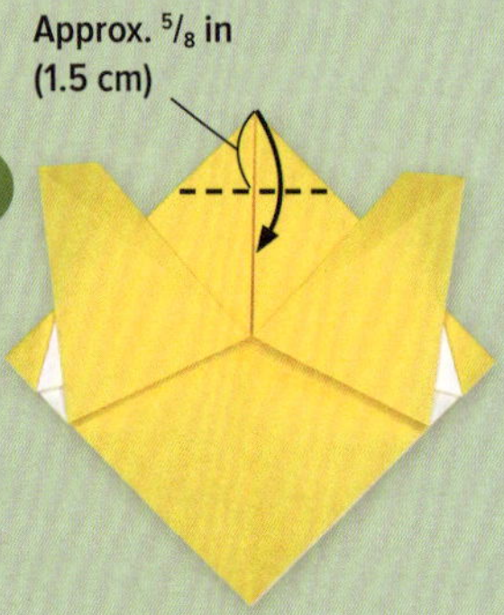

**8** Fold up 1 layer along the ○-to-○ span.

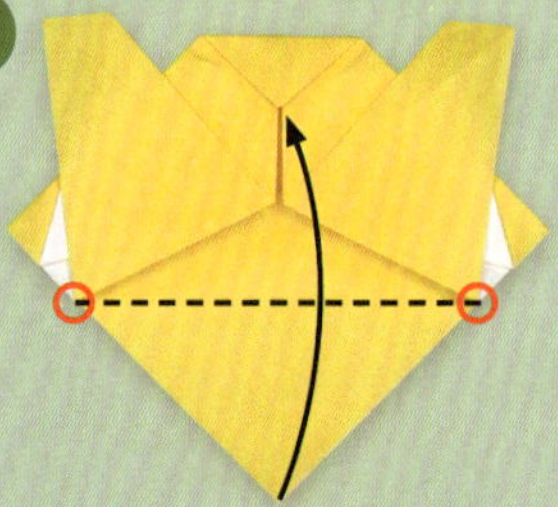

**9** Fold the corner as indicated. (Approx. 3⁄16 in (5 mm))

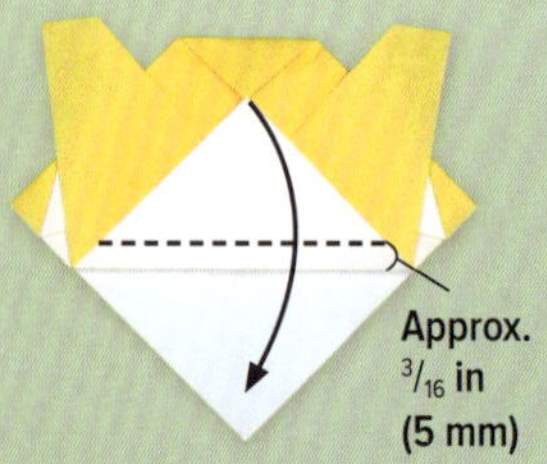

**10** Step 9 is completed. Flip it over.

**11** Fold the bottom right edge to align with the existing crease.

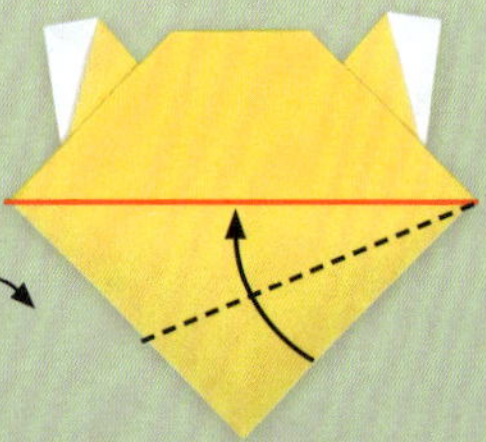

**12** Fold the bottom left edge to align with the existing crease.

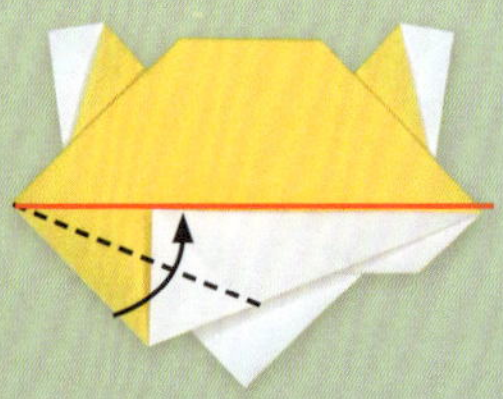

**13** Return to the state at the beginning of step 11.

48

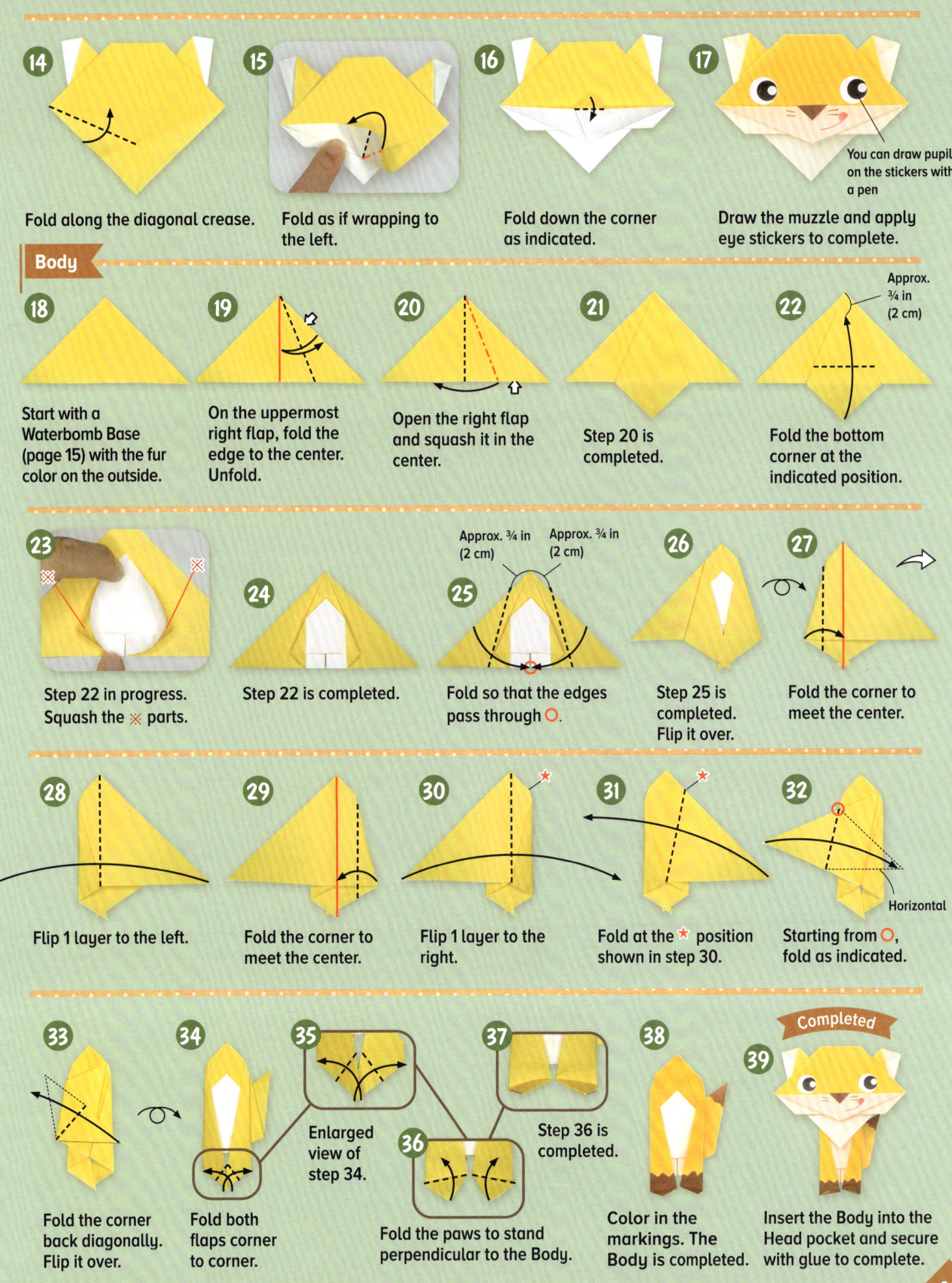

## ▶ FRIENDLY FOREST ANIMALS

# Mole
▶ Photo on page 6

VIDEO: tuttlepublishing.com/ unbelievably-cute-origami

Use a marker to finish by coloring my nose and the heaped soil brown.

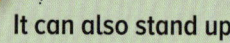
It can also stand up

- **Origami paper to use:** One 6-in (15-cm) sheet
- **Recommended tools:** Black felt tip pen, markers

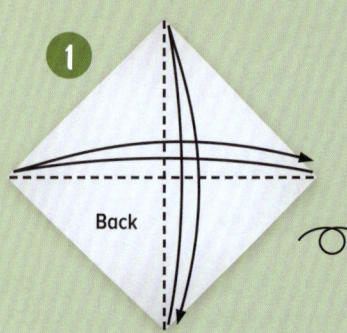
**1** Fold corner to corner both ways. Unfold after each. Flip it over.

**2** Fold the top corner to the center. Unfold.

**3** Fold the top corner to the step-2 crease. Unfold.

**4** Fold the top corner to the step-3 crease. Unfold.

**5** Fold the top corner to the step-4 crease.

**6** Fold so that the step-4 crease aligns with the step-3 crease.

**7** Step 6 is completed. Flip it over.

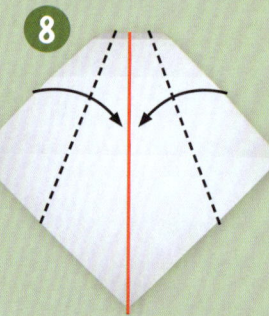
**8** Fold the top diagonal edges to the center.

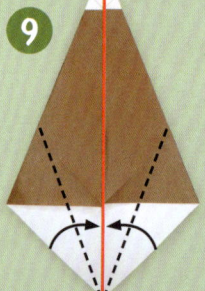
**9** Fold the bottom diagonal edges to the center.

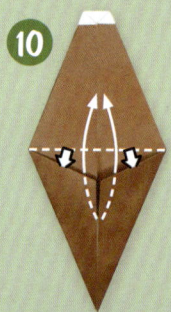
**10** Pull the hidden corners out, pivot them up, and squash them.

**11** Step 10 in progress.

**12** Step 10 is completed. Flip it over.

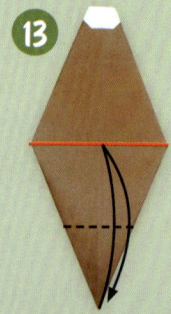
**13** Fold the bottom corner to the crease. Unfold.

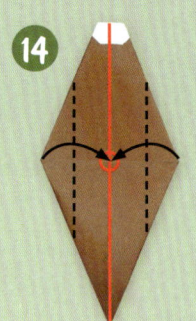
**14** Fold each side corner to the center.

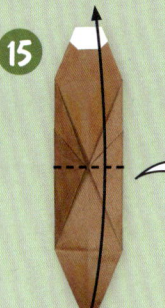
**15** Fold up along the existing crease.

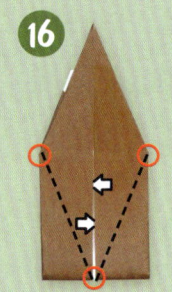
**16** Open the layers slightly and fold along the lines connecting the 2 side ○ points with the bottom.

**17** Fold the newly 3D corner down to the bottom, squashing the sides as you go.

**18** Step 17 is completed.

**19** From behind, swing the top section downward.

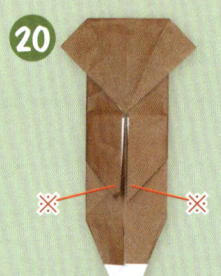
**20** Open the 2 marked flaps ✕ to the sides.

**21** The appearance of the paper after opening.

**22** Fold the marked area ✕ to the back while re-collapsing the shape into its previous form.

**23** Step 22 is completed.

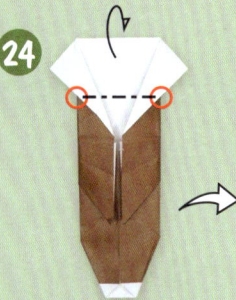
**24** Mountain fold along the ○-to-○ span.

**25** Step 24 is completed. Rotate the piece 180°.

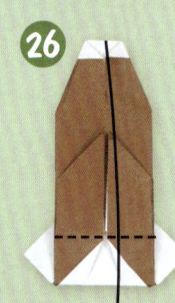
**26** Fold along the existing crease.

**27** Open the layers slightly and tuck the marked part ✕ inside.

**28** Step 27 is completed. Flip and rotate the piece.

**29** Fold the 2 flaps down at an angle.

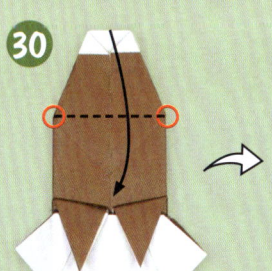
**30** Fold down along the ○-to-○ span.

**31** Fold small portions of the corners to the back side. Flip it over.

**32** If you want the model to stand up, open the ⇩⇩ area and adjust the angle. Flip it over.

**Completed**
**33** Color in the white areas with brown and draw on the face. It's completed!

51

▶ **FRIENDLY FOREST ANIMALS**

# Hedgehog
▶ Photo on page 7

VIDEO:
tuttlepublishing.com/
unbelievably-cute-origami

*I'm a little tricky to fold, but don't let that stop you!*

Large

Small

▸ **Origami paper to use:** Large: One 6-in (15-cm) sheet; Small: One 3-in (7.5-cm) sheet
▸ **Recommended tools:** Black felt tip pen, white paint pen

➔ The following instructions show 6-in (15-cm) origami paper being used.

**1**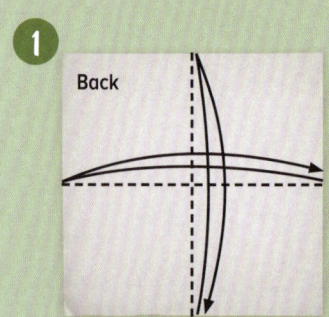
Fold edge to edge both ways. Unfold after each. Flip it over.

**2**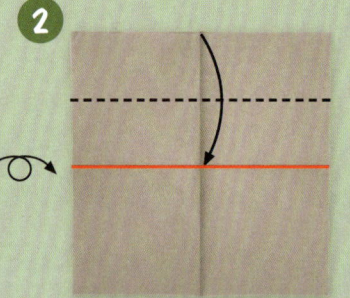
Fold the top edge to meet the center crease. Flip it over.

**3**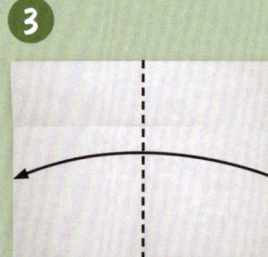
Fold the paper in half right edge to left edge.

**4**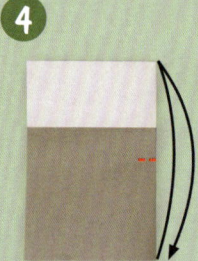
Bring the bottom edge up to the top edge and pinch to create a landmark.

**5**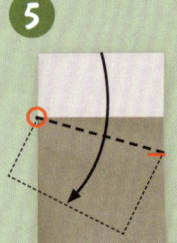
Fold along the span between the pinch mark and the ○ point.

**6**
Crease firmly
Step 5 is completed. Return the paper to the state at the beginning of step 3 shape.

**7**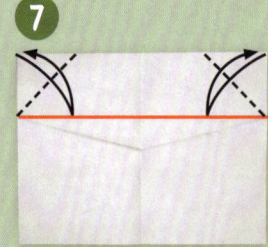
Fold the top corners to meet the step-1 central horizontal crease. Unfold both.

**8**
Inside reverse fold the corners along the creases from step 7.

**9**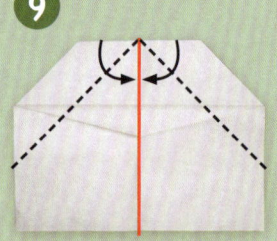
Fold the segments of the top edge down to align with the step-1 central vertical crease.

**10**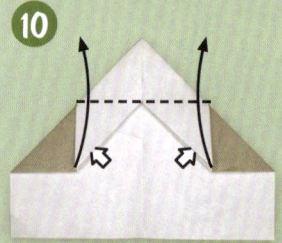
Fold up the triangular flaps of the uppermost layer.

**11**
Fold the corner down to the bottom edge.

**12**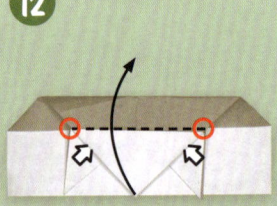
Fold the uppermost triangular flap up along the ○-to-○ span.

**13**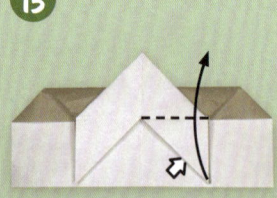
Fold the triangular flap up along the existing crease.

**14** Fold the corner to meet the ○ point.

**15** Fold the corner as indicated.

**16** Fold so that the corner protrudes slightly.

**17** Step 16 is completed.

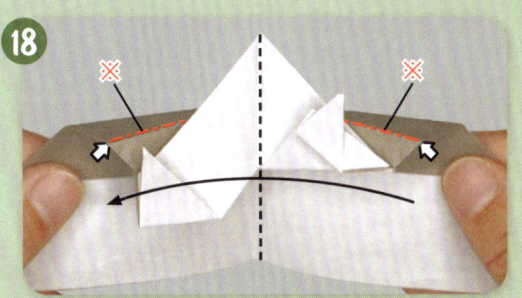
**18** Mountain fold along the step-5 creases (marked ✖) and fold the paper in half to collapse the shape.

**19** Step 18 is completed. Open the paper to the step-17 state.

**20** Pull the corner downward, and push the ○ part from the back.

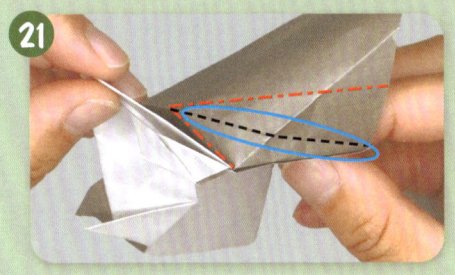
**21** Invert crease ◯ to a valley and then squash, forming a new mountain crease that extends to the edge.

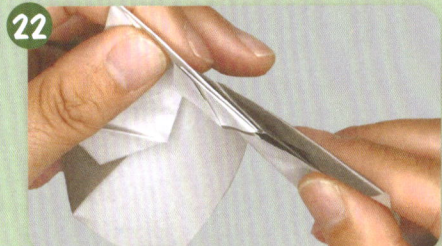
**22** Step 21 in progress.

**23** Step 22 is completed. Mirror steps 20–21 on the left side.

**24** Step 23 is completed.

**25** Fold the flaps to meet the diagonal edges.

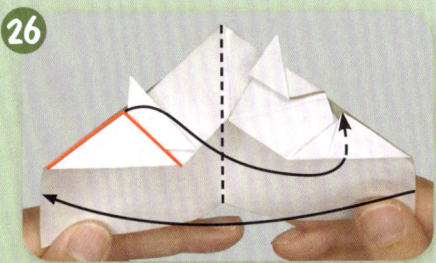
**26** Close the paper from right to left, and insert the left triangular flap into the pocket on the right to lock the shape.

**27** Rotate the model 90° counterclockwise.

**28** Make 2 mountain folds.

**Completed**
**29** Draw on the face and quill pattern. It's completed!

▶ FRIENDLY FOREST ANIMALS

# Owl
▶ Photo on page 7

VIDEO:
tuttlepublishing.com/
unbelievably-cute-origami

Draw an upside-down triangle pattern for my feathers using markers.

Large

Small

It's also cute to line up Owls folded from 6-in (15-cm) paper on the Tree Trunk (page 46) as decoration.

▶ **Origami paper to use:** Large: One 6-in (15-cm) sheet; Small: One 3-in (7.5-cm) sheet
▶ **Recommended tools:** Black felt tip pen, markers

➡ The following instructions show 6-in (15-cm) origami paper being used.

**1**
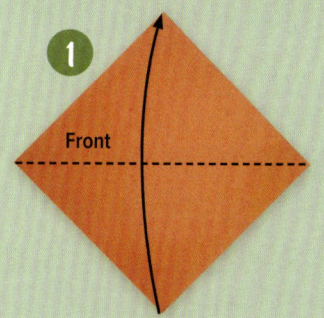
Fold the paper in half corner to corner.

**2**
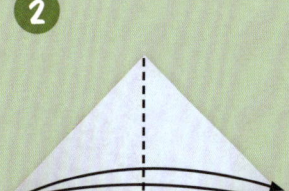
Fold corner to corner. Unfold.

**3**
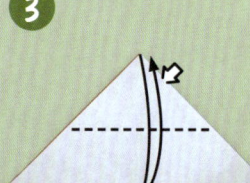
Fold the uppermost layer of the top corner to the bottom edge. Unfold.

**4**
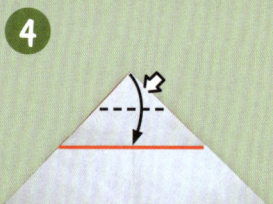
Fold the uppermost layer of the top corner to the step-3 crease.

**5**

Fold the corner to meet the edge formed in step 4.

**6**

Step 5 is completed. Flip it over.

**7**

Fold corner to corner so that the paired ○ points meet.

**8**

Fold the triangular regions edge to edge to bisect the angles. Unfold both.

**9**

Open the paper back to the state at the beginning of step 7.

**10**
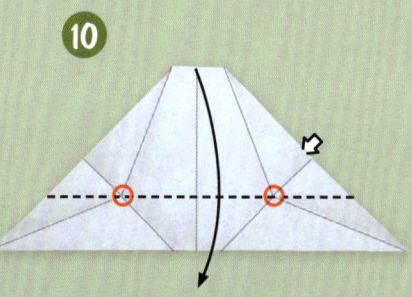
Fold the uppermost layer down along the path that runs through the ○ points.

**11**
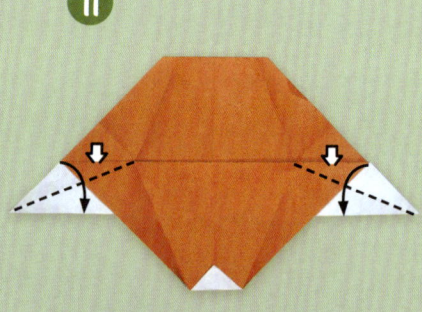
Fold the narrow triangular flaps to meet the bottom edge.

**12**

Fold along the existing crease to tuck the free edge to the back.

**13**

Step 12 in progress.

**14**

Step 12 is completed. Mirror step 12 on the left side.

**15**

Step 14 is completed. Flip it over.

**16**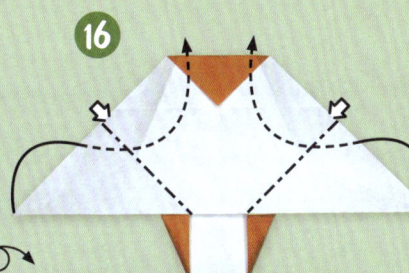

Inside reverse fold along the existing creases.

**17**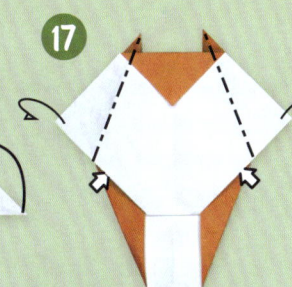

Mountain fold along the existing creases, tucking the flaps inside.

**18**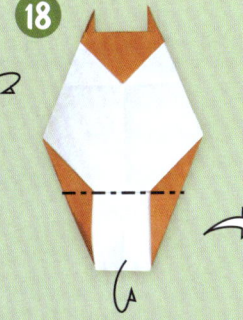

Mountain fold to the back along the edge.

**19**

Fold small portions of the corners inside.

**20**

Step 19 is completed. Flip it over.

**21**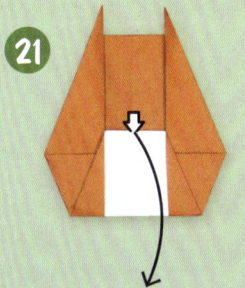

Swing open the flap. Look ahead to the shape in step 22.

**22**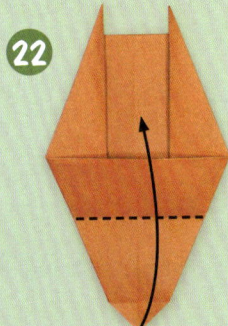

Fold up along the existing crease.

**23**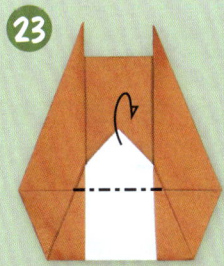

Mountain fold at the indicated position and tuck the flap inside.

**24**

Fold small portions of the protruding corners at mirroring angles to form the tufts.

**25**

Step 24 is completed. Flip it over.

**Completed**

**26**

Apply round eye stickers and color in the feather pattern to complete!

55

▶ FRIENDLY FOREST ANIMALS

# Squirrel
▶ Photo on page 6

VIDEO:
tuttlepublishing.com/
unbelievably-cute-origami

My cheeks are crammed with acorns and everything is right with the world!

- **Origami paper to use:** Head: One 6-in (15-cm) sheet / Body: One 6-in (15-cm) sheet
- **Recommended tools:** Black felt tip pen, white paint pen, markers, round stickers (black, 3/16 in / 5 mm), glue or masking tape

## Head

**1**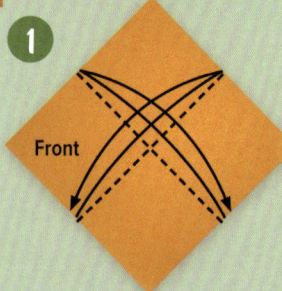
Fold edge to edge both ways. Unfold after each.

**2**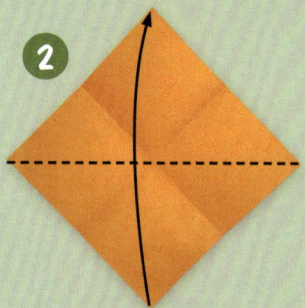
Fold the paper in half corner to corner.

**3**
One at a time, fold the side edges of the uppermost layer to the bottom edge, only along the marked positions. Unfold after each.

**4**
Step 3 in progress.

**5**
Step 3 is completed. Flip it over.

**6**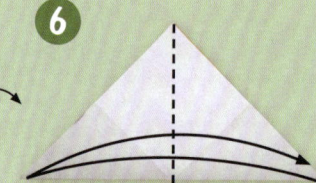
Fold corner to corner. Unfold.

**7**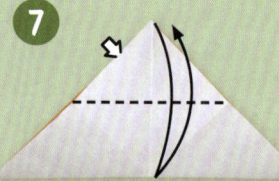
Fold the uppermost layer of the top corner to the bottom edge. Unfold.

**8**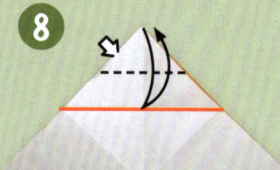
Fold the uppermost layer of the top corner to the step-7 crease. Unfold.

**9**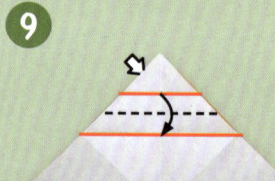
Fold so that the crease made in step 8 meets the crease made in step 7.

**10**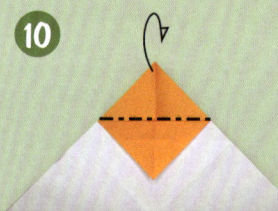
Fold the corner of the lowermost layer back along the edge formed in step 9.

**11**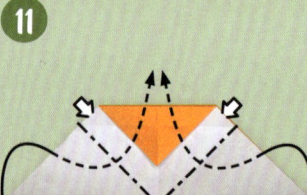
Inside reverse fold along the existing creases.

**12**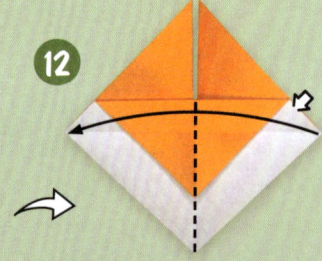
Flip 1 layer to the left.

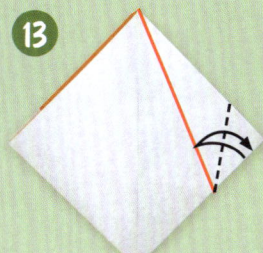
**13** Fold the edge to meet the step-3 crease. Unfold.

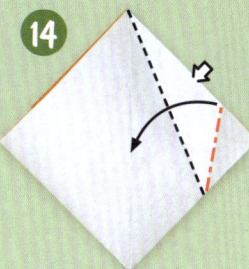
**14** Open slightly and squash along the existing creases.

**15** Fold the upper left edge of the uppermost flap to the center. Unfold.

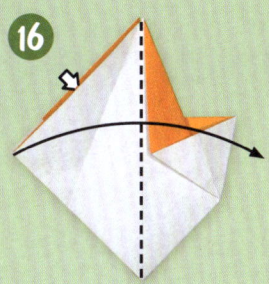
**16** Flip 1 layer to the right.

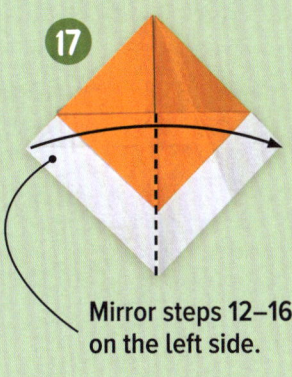
**17** Mirror steps 12–16 on the left side.

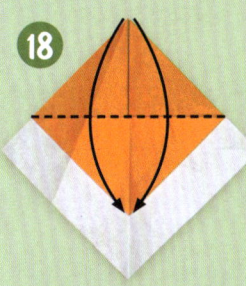
**18** Step 17 is completed. Fold the flaps down along the edge.

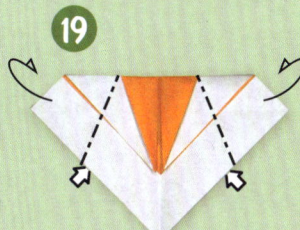
**19** Open slightly and fold the uppermost flaps to the inside along the existing creases.

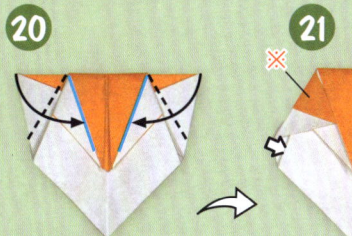
**20** Fold the corners to align with the edges of the colored region.

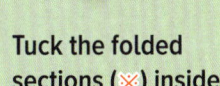
**21** Tuck the folded sections (✖) inside.

**22** Fold the flaps up diagonally to form the ears.

**23** Fold the bottom corner up at the indicated point ◯.

**24** Tuck the step-23 flap (✖) inside.

**25** Flip it over.

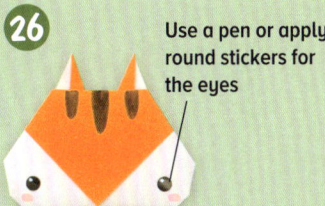
**26** Use a pen or apply round stickers for the eyes

Draw on the face and color in the coat markings. The Head is completed.

## Body

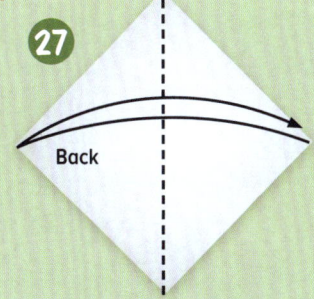
**27** Fold the paper in half corner to corner. Unfold.

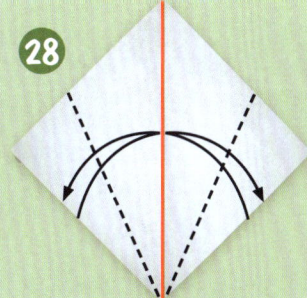
**28** Fold the bottom edges to the center. Unfold both.

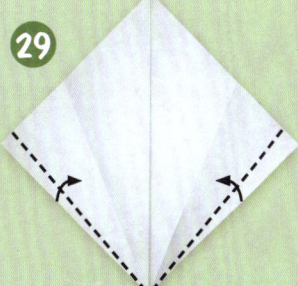
**29** Fold in small portions of both bottom edges.

**30** Refold along the step-28 creases.

57

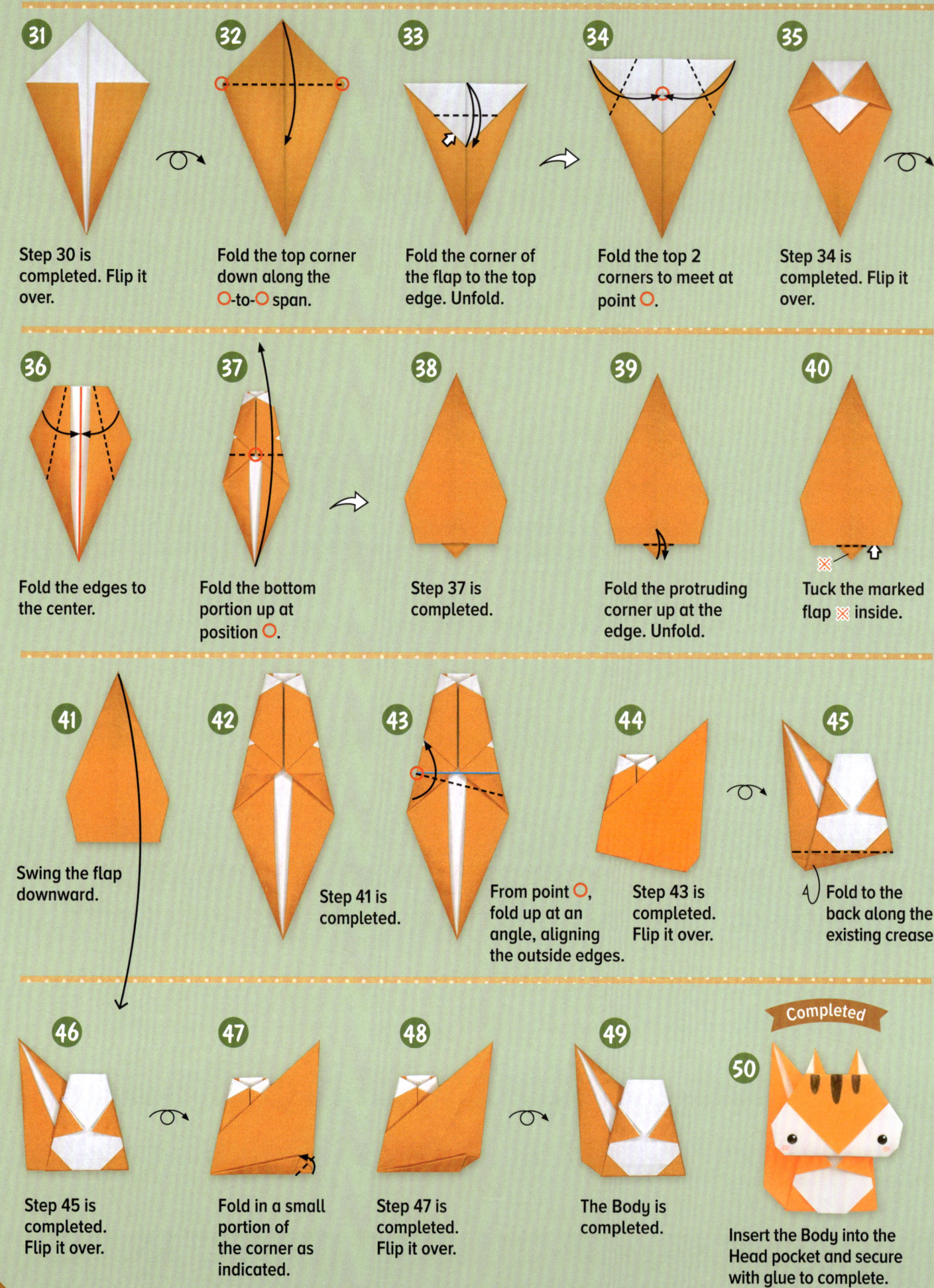

▶ FRIENDLY FOREST ANIMALS

# Japanese Snow Fairy
▶ Photo on page 7

VIDEO: tuttlepublishing.com/ unbelievably-cute-origami

I can be used to make a decorative display by perching on the Tree Trunk (page 46)!

Large
Small
It can also stand up

- **Origami paper to use:** Large: One 6-in (15-cm) sheet; Small: One 3-in (7.5-cm) sheet
- **Recommended tools:** Black felt tip pen or marker

➔ The following instructions show 6-in (15-cm) origami paper being used.

**1** Fold corner to corner both ways. Unfold after each. Flip it over.

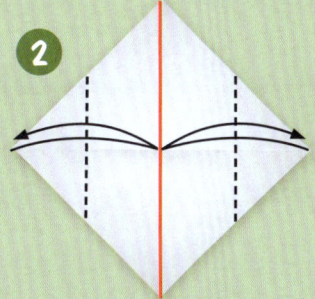
**2** Fold the side corners to the center. Unfold both.

**3** Fold the edges to meet the step-2 creases.

**4** Refold along the step-2 creases.

**5** Step 4 is completed. Flip it over.

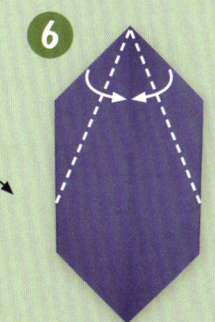
**6** Fold the edges to the center.

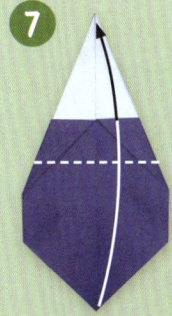
**7** Fold along the existing crease.

**8** Fold as indicated.

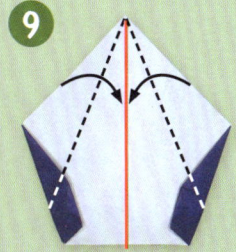
**9** Fold the edges to the center.

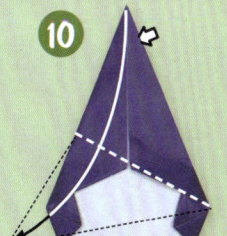
**10** Fold the uppermost flap down at an angle to meet a point extending horizontally from the bottom edge.

**11** Fold the flap along the existing crease.

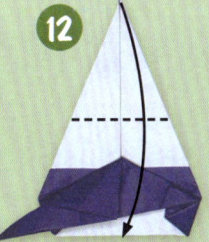
**12** Fold the corner to meet the bottom edge.

**13** Fold in small portions of the top corners. Flip it over.

**14** Completed
Draw on the face to complete.

▶ FRIENDLY FOREST ANIMALS

# Bumblebee
Photo on page 6

VIDEO:
tuttlepublishing.com/
unbelievably-cute-origami

Create two wings using a single sheet of origami paper, without cutting!

Large

Small

- **Origami paper to use:** Large: One 6-in (15-cm) sheet; Small: One 3-in (7.5-cm) sheet
- **Recommended tools:** black felt tip pen, markers, round stickers

➡ The following instructions show 6-in (15-cm) origami paper being used.

**1**
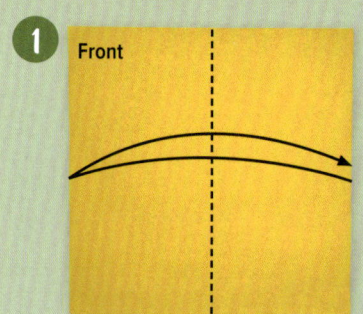
Fold the paper in half edge to edge. Unfold.

**2**
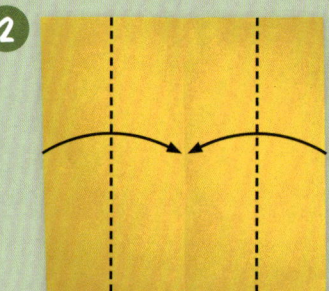
Fold the edges to align with the crease.

**3**
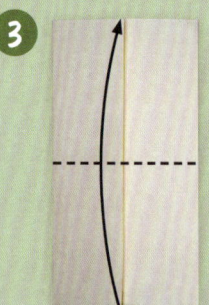
Fold the bottom edge to the top edge.

**4**
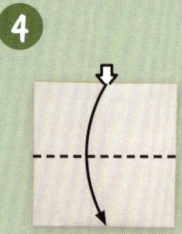
Fold the uppermost flap down to the bottom edge.

**5**

Unfold the paper completely.

**6**

Flip it over.

**7**
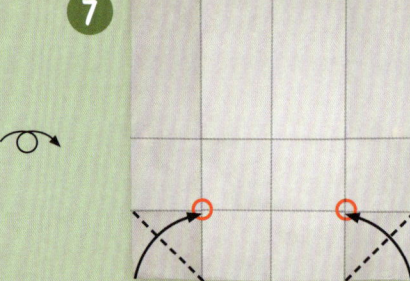
Fold the bottom corners to the ○ crease intersections.

**8**
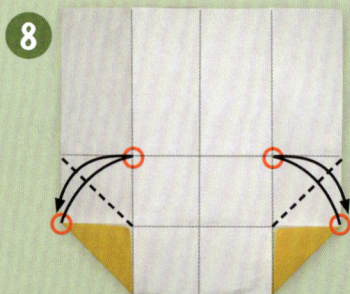
Fold so that the paired ○ points meet in 2 locations. Unfold after each.

**9**

Step 8 is completed. Flip it over.

**10**
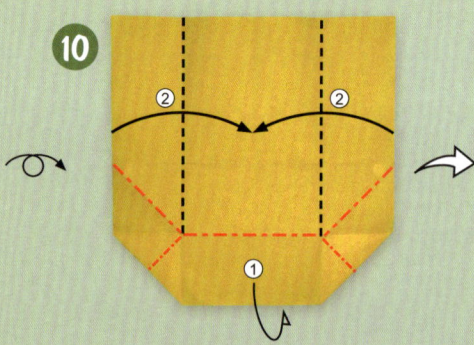
Fold in the order of steps ①, then ②.

11
Step 10 is completed.

12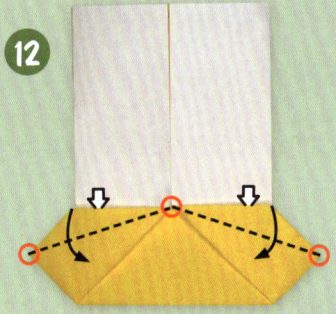
Fold along the ○-to-○ spans.

13
Fold the bottom edge up along the existing crease indicated by the ○-to-○ span.

14
Step 13 is completed. Flip it over.

15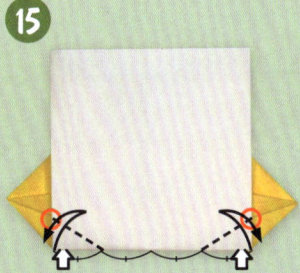
Fold both bottom corners of the uppermost flap as indicated from the ○ points. Unfold both.

16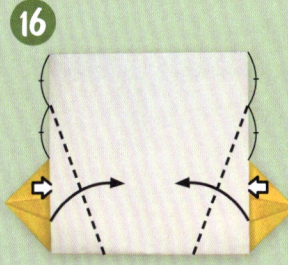
Fold the sides in as indicated, squashing pockets that open up along the step-15 creases.

17
Fold the top edge of the top layer to meet the ○-to-○ span, squashing the pocket that opens up at each end.

18
Step 17 in progress. Open up pockets on both sides.

19
Step 17 is completed. The triangular pockets have been squashed.

20
Fold in 3 corners.

21
Step 20 is completed. Flip it over.

22 **Completed**
Apply round eye stickers, draw on the mouth and wing veins, and color in the abdominal stripes to complete.

61

▶ **COOL AQUATIC & WATERSIDE ANIMALS**

# Dolphin
▶ Photo on page 8

VIDEO: tuttlepublishing.com/unbelievably-cute-origami

With a curved pose, I appear to be gracefully breaching above the surf.

- ▶ **Origami paper to use:** One 6-in (15-cm) sheet
- ▶ **Recommended tools:** Scissors, round stickers (black, 3/16 in / 5 mm)

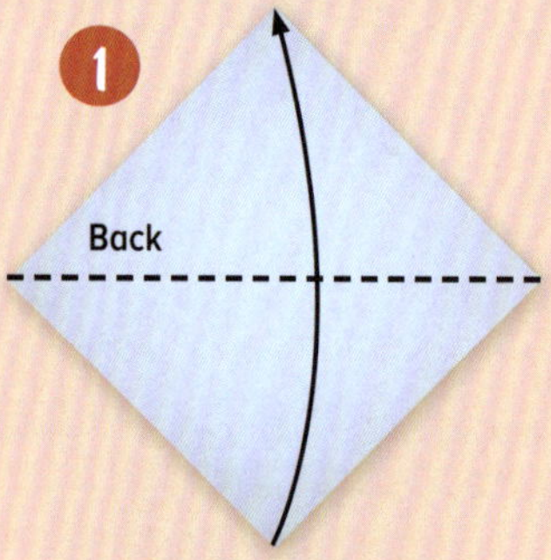

**1** Back
Fold the paper in half corner to corner.

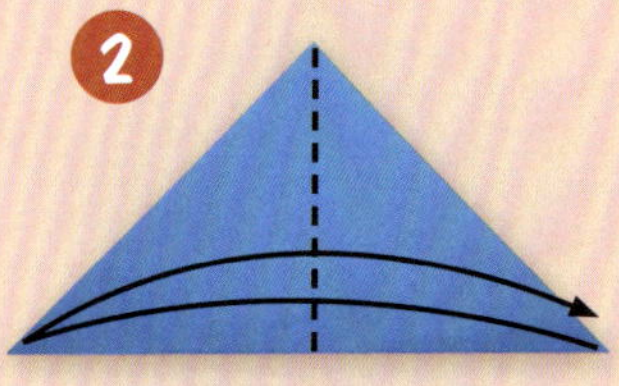

**2** Fold corner to corner. Unfold.

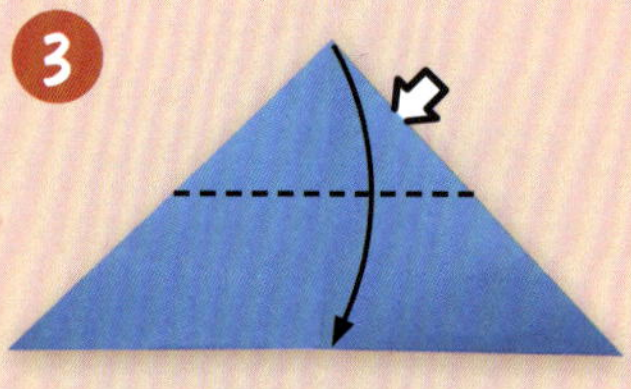

**3** Fold the uppermost layer of the top corner to the bottom edge.

**4** Step 3 is completed. Flip it over.

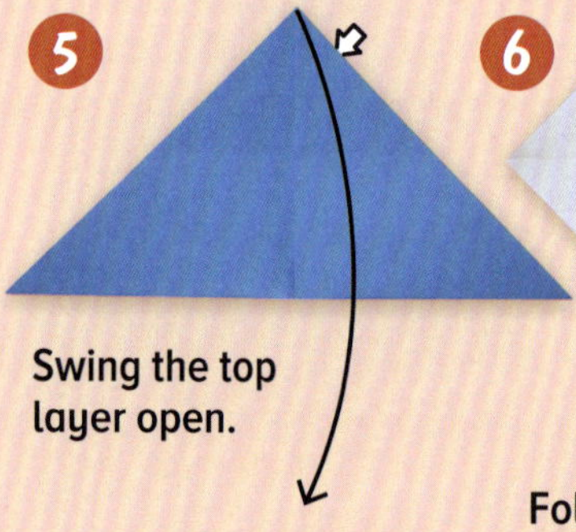

**5** Swing the top layer open.

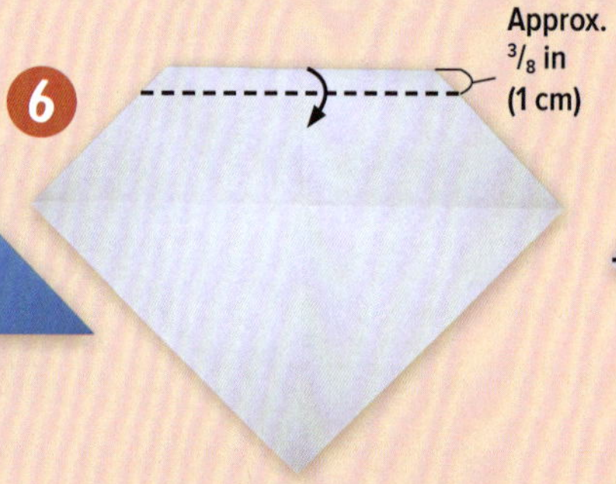

**6** Approx. 3/8 in (1 cm)
Fold a small strip of the top edge down as indicated.

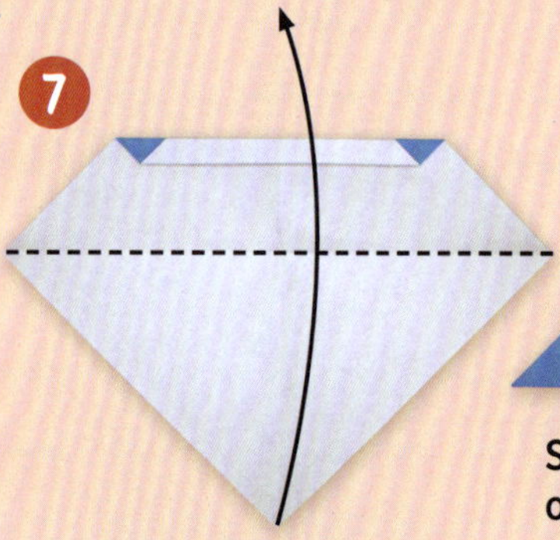

**7** Fold the flap up along the existing crease.

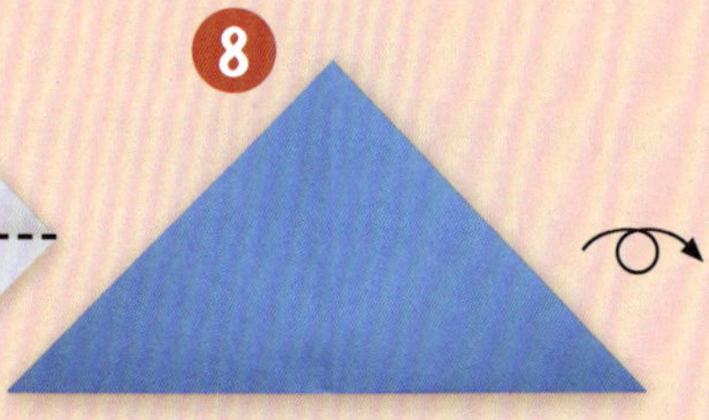

**8** Step 7 is completed. Flip it over.

**9** Fold the corner of the lowermost layer back along the edge formed in step 6.

**10** Step 9 is completed. Flip it over.

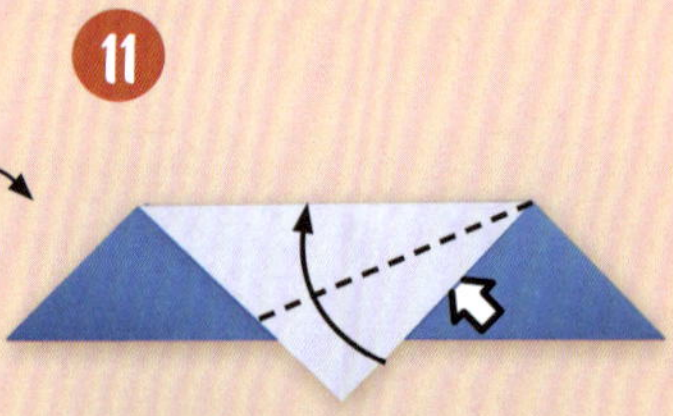

**11** Bisect the angle by folding the right diagonal flap edge to meet the top edge.

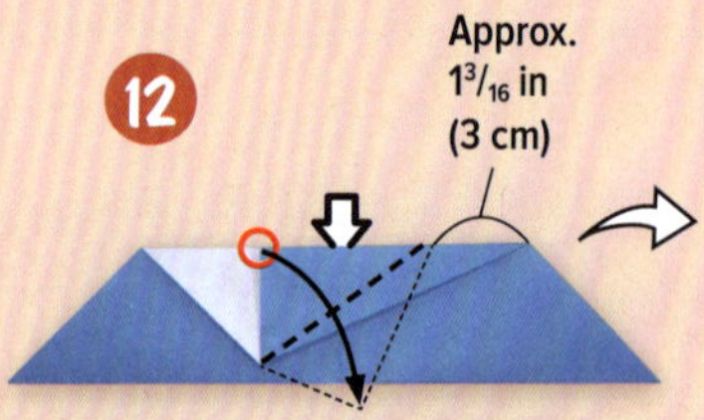

**12** Approx. 1 3/16 in (3 cm)
Fold the flap diagonally as indicated so that point ○ protrudes slightly at the bottom.

62

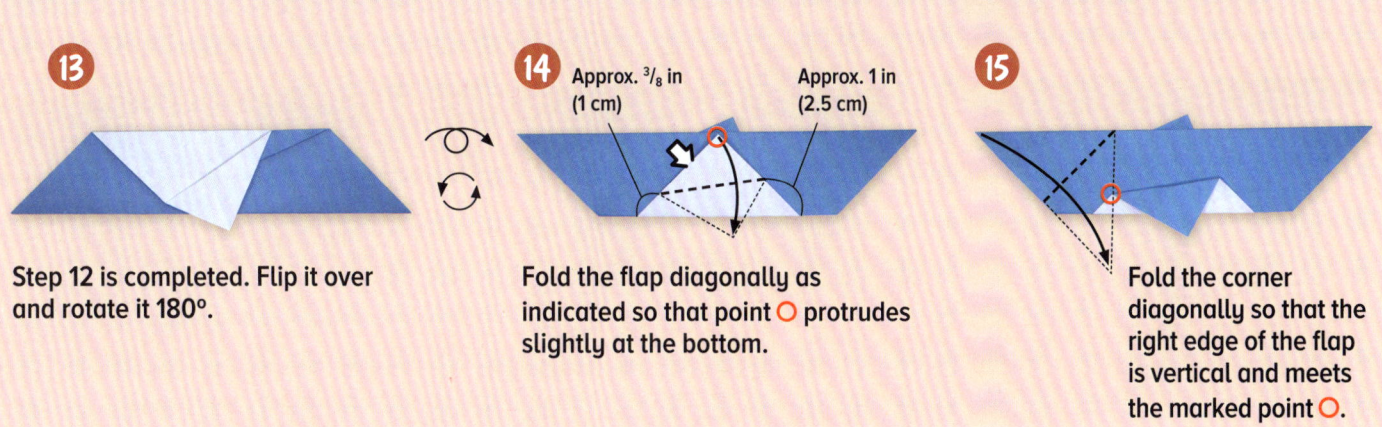

**13** Step 12 is completed. Flip it over and rotate it 180°.

**14** Approx. 3/8 in (1 cm). Approx. 1 in (2.5 cm). Fold the flap diagonally as indicated so that point ○ protrudes slightly at the bottom.

**15** Fold the corner diagonally so that the right edge of the flap is vertical and meets the marked point ○.

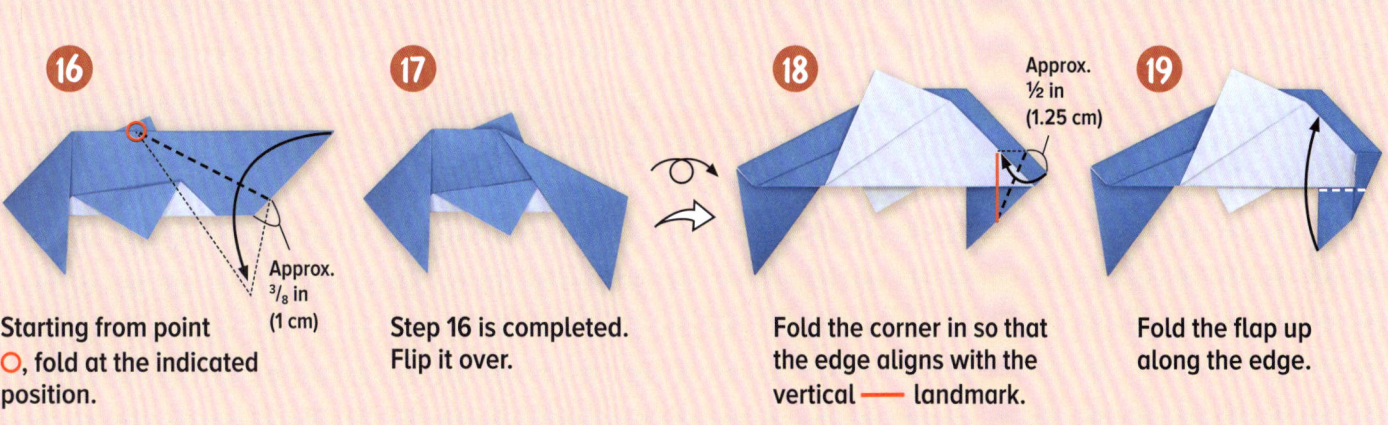

**16** Starting from point ○, fold at the indicated position. Approx. 3/8 in (1 cm)

**17** Step 16 is completed. Flip it over.

**18** Fold the corner in so that the edge aligns with the vertical — landmark.

**19** Approx. ½ in (1.25 cm). Fold the flap up along the edge.

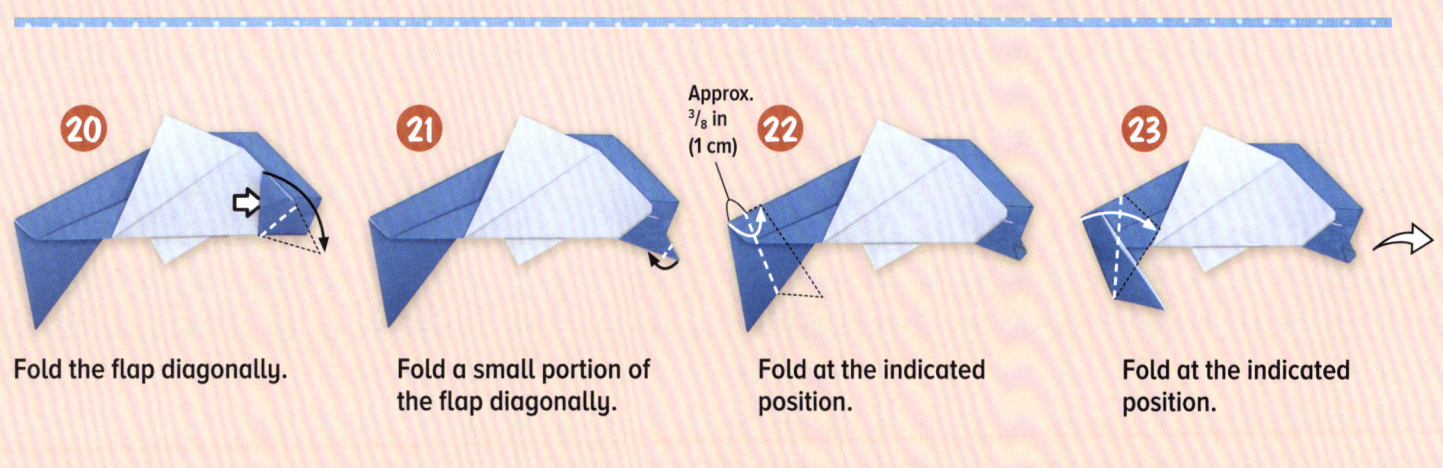

**20** Fold the flap diagonally.

**21** Fold a small portion of the flap diagonally.

**22** Approx. 3/8 in (1 cm). Fold at the indicated position.

**23** Fold at the indicated position.

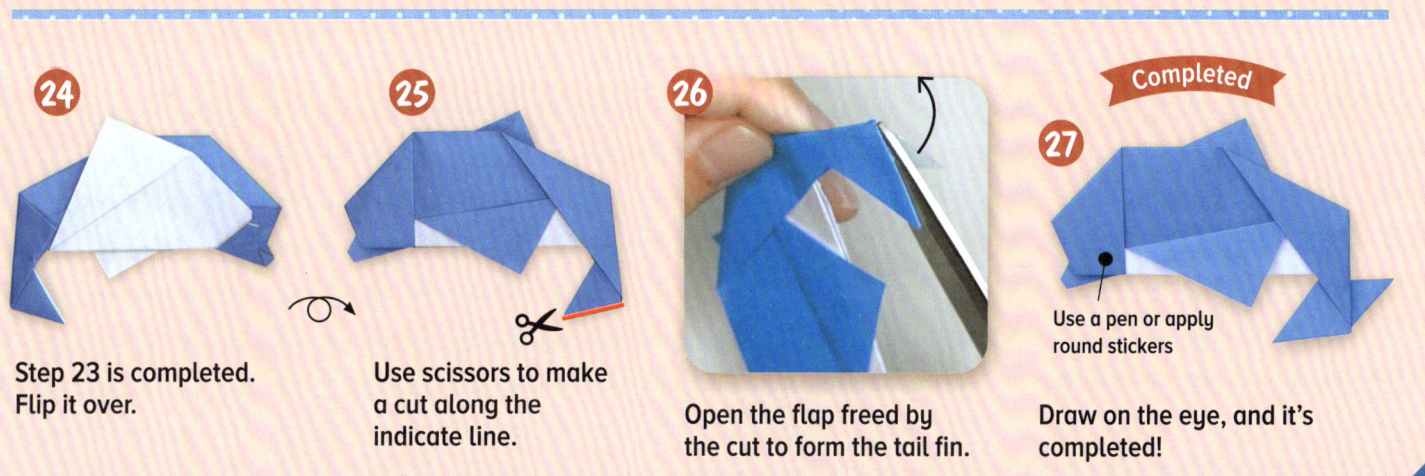

**24** Step 23 is completed. Flip it over.

**25** Use scissors to make a cut along the indicate line.

**26** Open the flap freed by the cut to form the tail fin.

**27** Completed. Use a pen or apply round stickers. Draw on the eye, and it's completed!

▶ COOL AQUATIC & WATERSIDE ANIMALS

# Whale
▶ Photo on page 8

VIDEO:
tuttlepublishing.com/
unbelievably-cute-origami

"My large, round head makes it look like I'm about to spout a plume of spray at any moment. I'm super cute!"

Large

Small

- **Origami paper to use:** Large: One 6-in (15-cm) sheet; Small: One 3-in (7.5-cm) sheet
- **Recommended tools:** Black felt tip pen, white paint pen, round stickers (for Large: black, 5/8 in / 1.5 cm; for Small: white, 5/16 in / 8 mm)
→ The following instructions show 6-in (15-cm) origami paper being used.

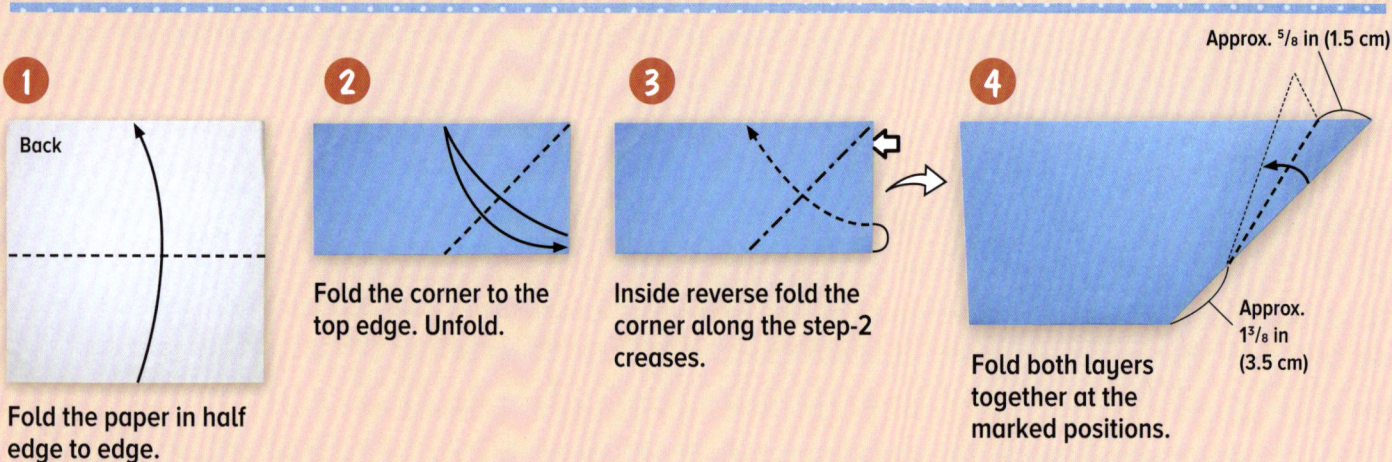

**1** Fold the paper in half edge to edge.

**2** Fold the corner to the top edge. Unfold.

**3** Inside reverse fold the corner along the step-2 creases.

**4** Fold both layers together at the marked positions. Approx. 5/8 in (1.5 cm) / Approx. 1 3/8 in (3.5 cm)

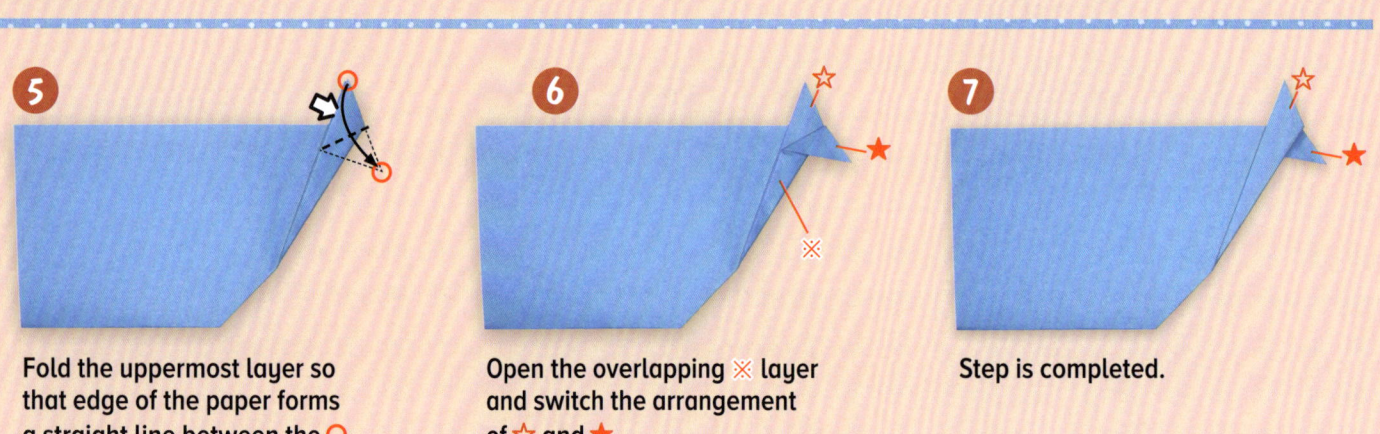

**5** Fold the uppermost layer so that edge of the paper forms a straight line between the ○ points.

**6** Open the overlapping ※ layer and switch the arrangement of ☆ and ★.

**7** Step is completed.

**8** Swing flap ☆ to the inside by reversing the existing crease.

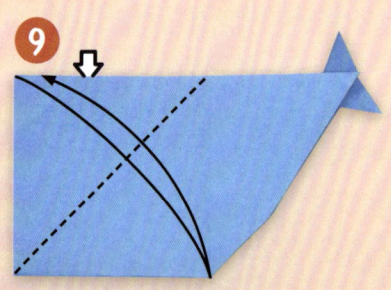
**9** Fold the uppermost layer corner to corner. Unfold.

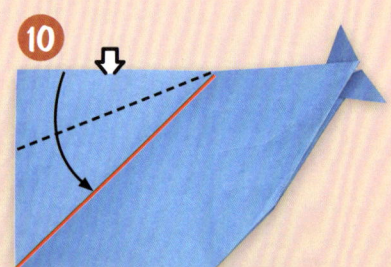
**10** Fold the top edge of the uppermost layer to meet the step-9 crease.

64

**11** Fold ★ to the back along the edge of the step-10 flap.

**12** Step 11 is completed. Flip it over and rotate it 180°.

**13** Open flap ☆.

**14** Fold the corner to the crease, folding in parallel to the existing crease.

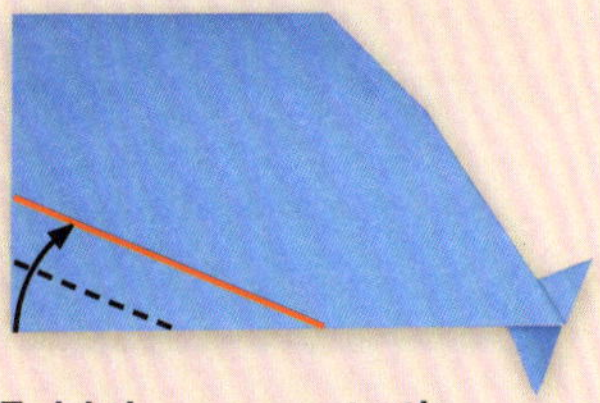

**15** Refold along the existing crease.

**16** Step 15 is completed. Flip it over.

**17** Fold along the marked path.

**18** Pull out and open the partially hidden flap ※.

**19** Step 18 is completed.

**20** Fold so that the paired ○ points meet.

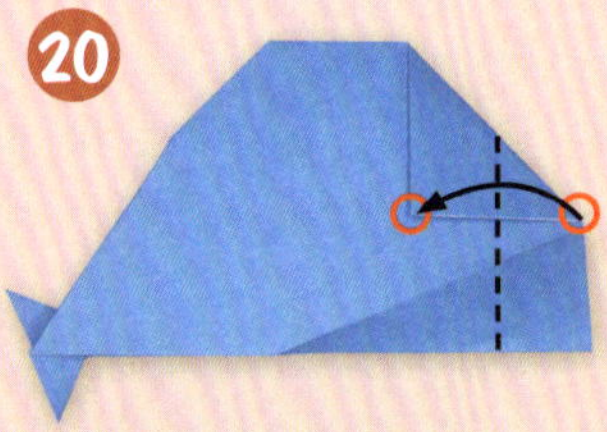

**21** Approx. 3/8 in (1 cm). Fold along the ○-to-○ span.

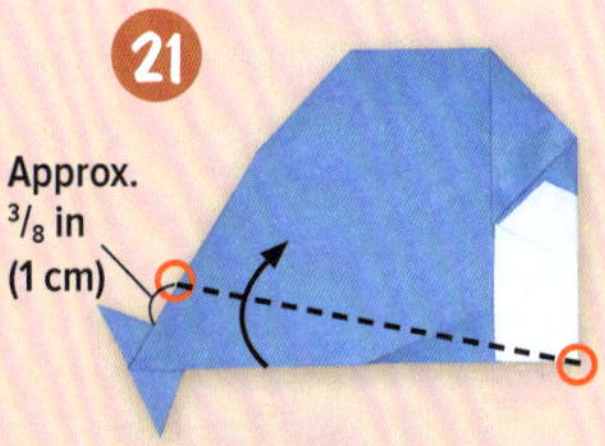

**22** Fold along the ○-to-○ span.

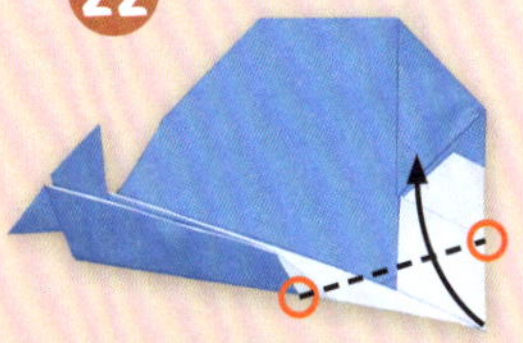

**23** Open the area folded in step 22.

**24** Open pocket ※ and insert flap ★ to secure it.

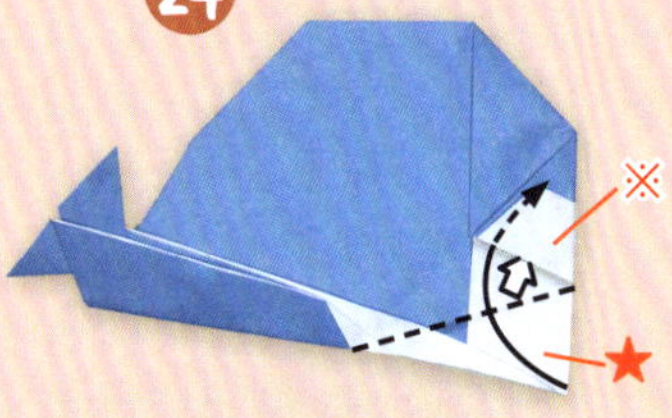

**25** Step 24 is completed. Flip it over.

**26** **Completed** You can draw pupils on the stickers with a pen. Apply the eye sticker, and it's completed!

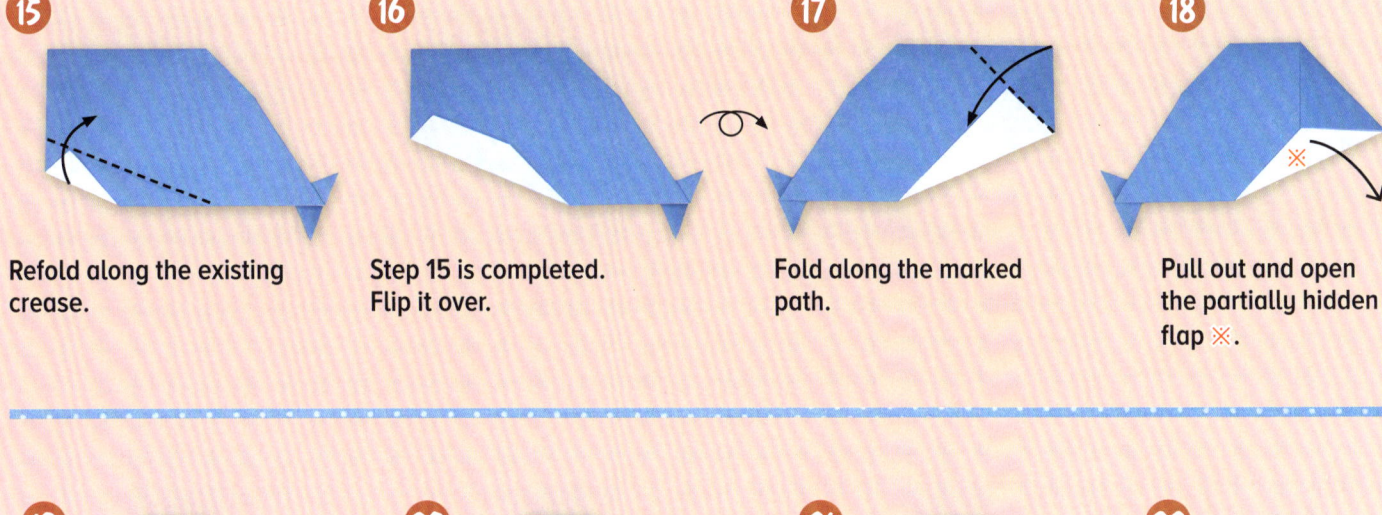

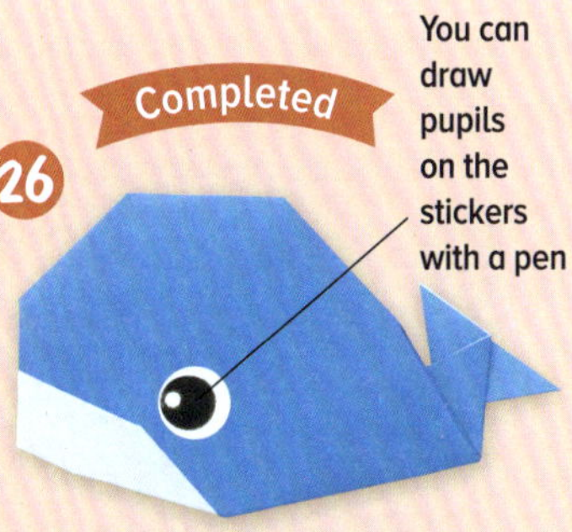

65

▶ COOL AQUATIC & WATERSIDE ANIMALS

# Penguin
▶ Photo on page 9

VIDEO:
tuttlepublishing.com/
unbelievably-cute-origami

My beak and feet are finished by coloring them yellow with a marker.

- **Origami paper to use:** One 6-in (15-cm) sheet
- **Recommended tools:** Black felt tip pen, white paint pen, colored pen, round stickers (black, 3/16 in / 5 mm)

**1**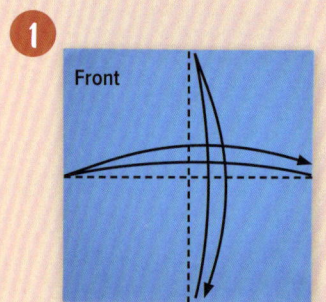
Fold edge to edge both ways. Unfold after each.

**2**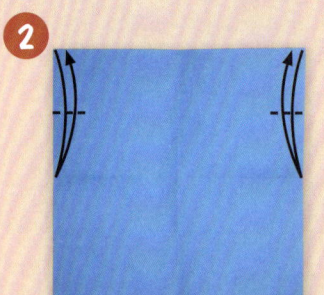
Bring the top edge to the center horizontal crease and pinch on either side to create landmarks.

**3**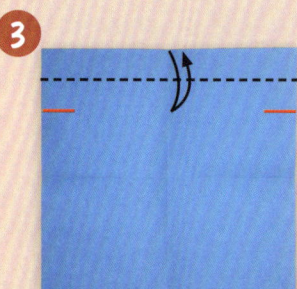
Fold the top edge to the pinch marks made in step 2. Unfold.

**4**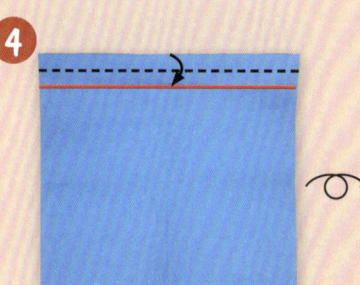
Fold the top edge to the step-3 crease. Flip it over left to right.

**5**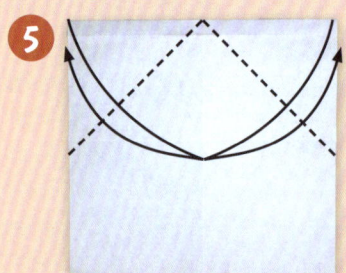
Fold the top corners to the center vertical crease. Unfold both.

**6**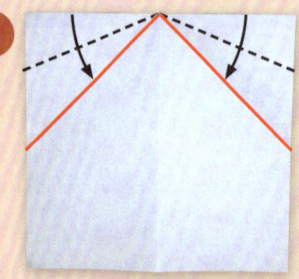
Fold equal segments of the top edge to meet the step-5 creases.

**7**
Fold along the existing creases.

**8**
Fold behind through all layers along the horizontal crease on the lowermost layer.

**9**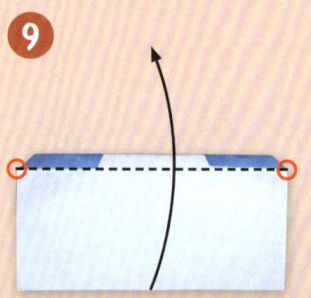
Fold the bottom portion of the paper up along the ○-to-○ span.

**10**
Step 9 is completed. Flip it over.

**11**
Fold the corner to meet the edge formed in step 9.

**12**
Step 11 is completed. Flip it over.

**13**
Pull out the flap marked ✕.

**14**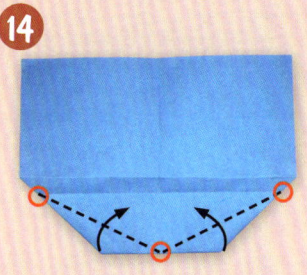
Fold along the ○-to-○ spans.

**15**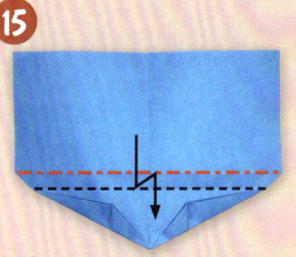
Push the step-folded flap opened in step 13 back into place.

**16**
Step 15 is completed. Flip it over.

**17**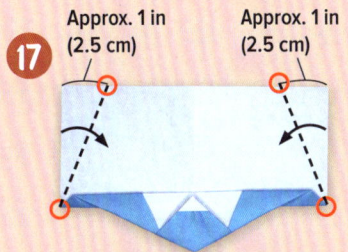
Approx. 1 in (2.5 cm)   Approx. 1 in (2.5 cm)
Fold the edges in along the ○-to-○ spans.

**18**
Step 17 is completed. Rotate the paper 180°.

**19**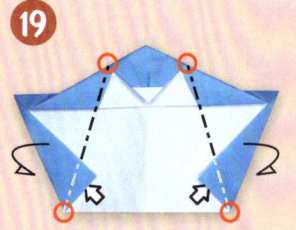
Fold toward the back along the ○-to-○ spans.

**20**
Step 19 is completed. Flip it over.

**21**
Fold the outside edges of the flaps to align with the bottom edge.

**22**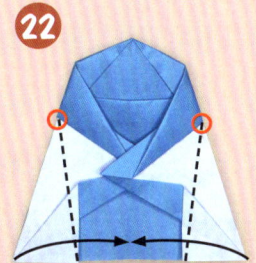
Starting from the ○ locations, fold the corners in to the center.

**23**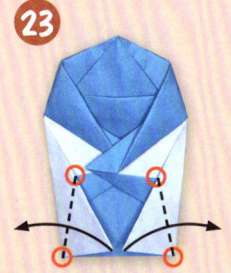
Fold the flaps out along the ○-to-○ spans.

**24**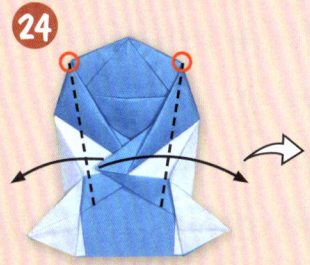
Starting from the ○ locations, fold the flaps so that they protrude to the outside.

**25**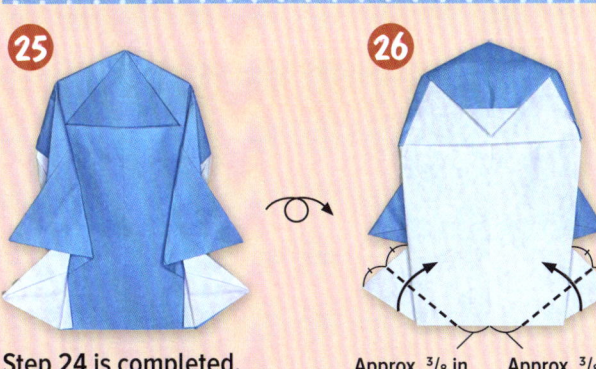
Step 24 is completed. Flip it over.

**26**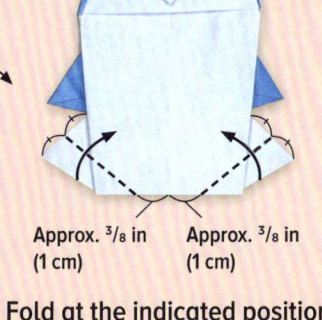
Approx. 3/8 in (1 cm)   Approx. 3/8 in (1 cm)
Fold at the indicated positions.

**27**
Fold to the back along the ○-to-○ span.

**28** **Completed**
Use a pen or apply round stickers
Color in the beak and feet, draw on the eyes, and it's completed!

▶ COOL AQUATIC & WATERSIDE ANIMALS

# Polar Bear
▶ Photo on page 9

VIDEO: tuttlepublishing.com/unbelievably-cute-origami

If you fold my paws forward, you can make me stand for display!

Standing version

Flat version

- **Origami paper to use:** One 6-in (15-cm) sheet
- **Recommended tool:** Black felt tip pen

**1** Fold corner to corner both ways. Unfold after each. Flip it over.

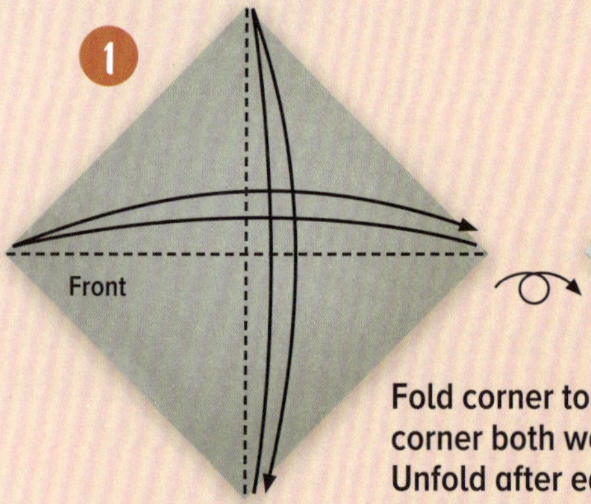

**2** Bring the top corner to the center and pinch to create a landmark.

**3** Bring the top corner to the step-2 mark and pinch again.

**4** Fold the top corner to the step-3 pinch mark. Unfold.

**5** Enlarged view of step 4.

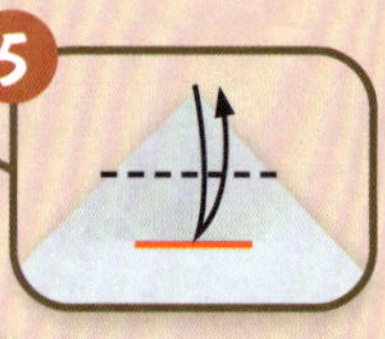

**6** Fold a small portion of the corner down, placing the crease at about 1/8 in (3 mm) from the top.

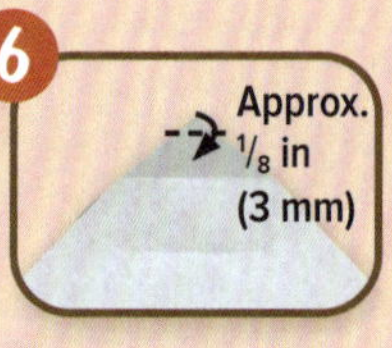

**7** Refold along the step-4 crease.

**8** Step 7 is completed.

**9** Make small mountain folds at the indicated positions.
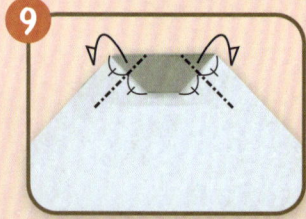

**10** Step 9 is completed.

**11** Flip it over.

**12** Fold the upper edges in at the indicated positions. Approx. 1 in (2.5 cm)
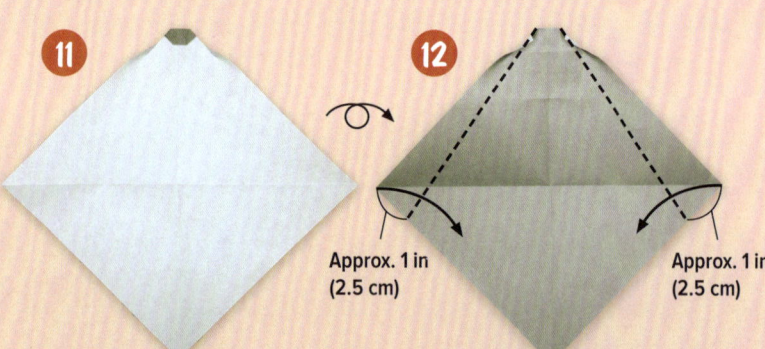

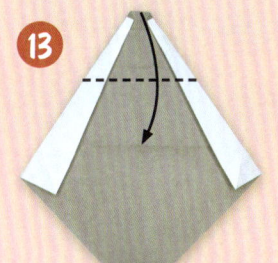

**13** Fold the top edge to the crease junction.

**14** Step 13 is completed. Open the 3 sections.

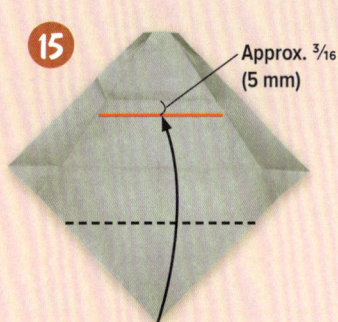

**15** Fold up the bottom corner so that it falls about 3/16 in (5 mm) short of the top crease. (Approx. 3/16 in (5 mm))

**16** Refold along the step-12 creases.

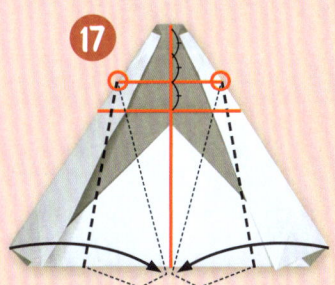

**17** Starting from the ○ locations, fold the corners to meet in the center just below the bottom edge.

**18** Step 17 is completed.

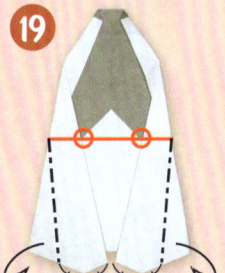

**19** Make mountain folds at the indicated positions.

**20** Step 19 is completed. Return the paper to the state in step 18.

**21** The flaps have been unfolded.

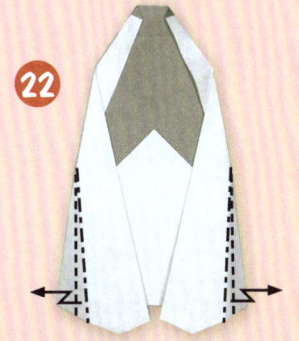

**22** Make staggered folds by slightly shifting the step-19 creases and squashing them.

**23** Fold along the existing crease.

**24** Mountain fold the top corners.

**25** Step 24 is completed. Flip it over.

**26** Fold small portions of the flaps out so that they protrude slightly beyond the edges.

**27** Step 26 is completed. Flip it over.

**28** The flat version is completed. Fold the paw flaps to stand perpendicular so that the model will stand up.

**29** Completed
Draw on the eyes, and it's completed!

▶ COOL AQUATIC & WATERSIDE ANIMALS

# Otter

▶ Photo on page 9

It can also stand up

- **Origami paper to use:** Large: One 6-in (15-cm) sheet; Small: One 4-in (10-cm) sheet
- **Recommended tool:** Black felt tip pen

→ The following instructions show 6-in (15-cm) origami paper being used.

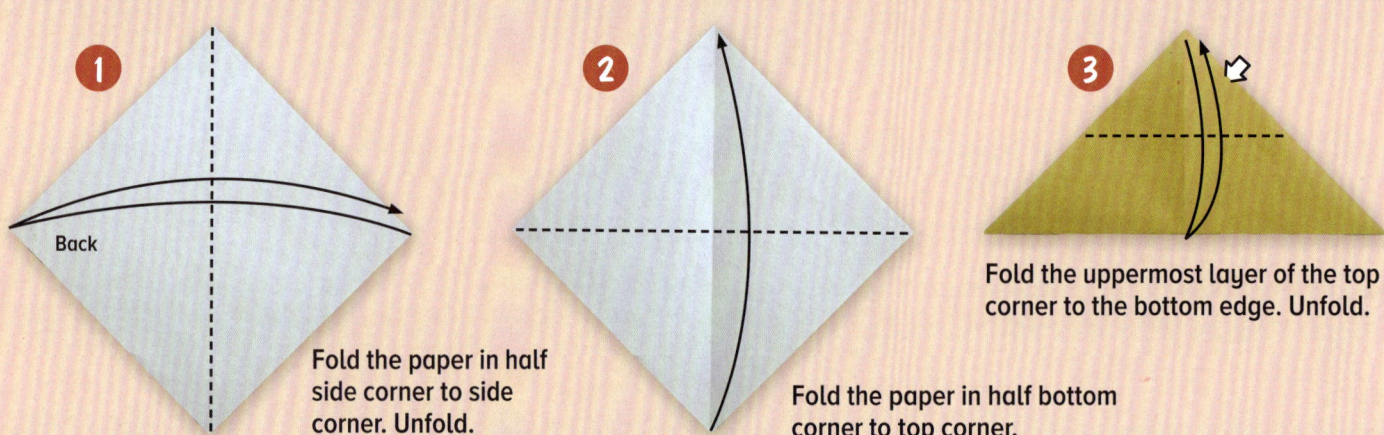

**1** Fold the paper in half side corner to side corner. Unfold.

**2** Fold the paper in half bottom corner to top corner.

**3** Fold the uppermost layer of the top corner to the bottom edge. Unfold.

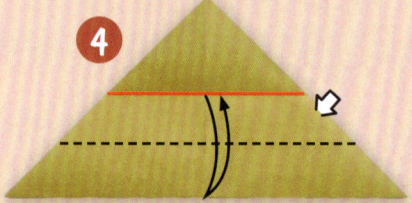

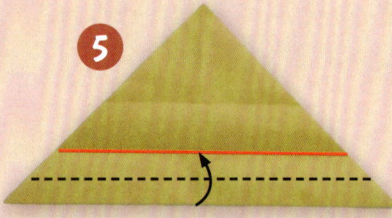

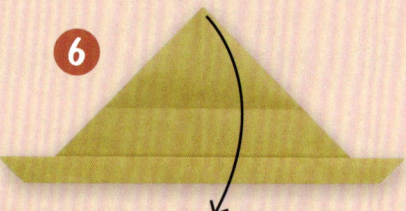

**4** Fold the uppermost layer so that the step-3 crease aligns with the bottom edge. Unfold.

**5** Fold the bottom edge up to the step-4 crease.

**6** Open the paper completely.

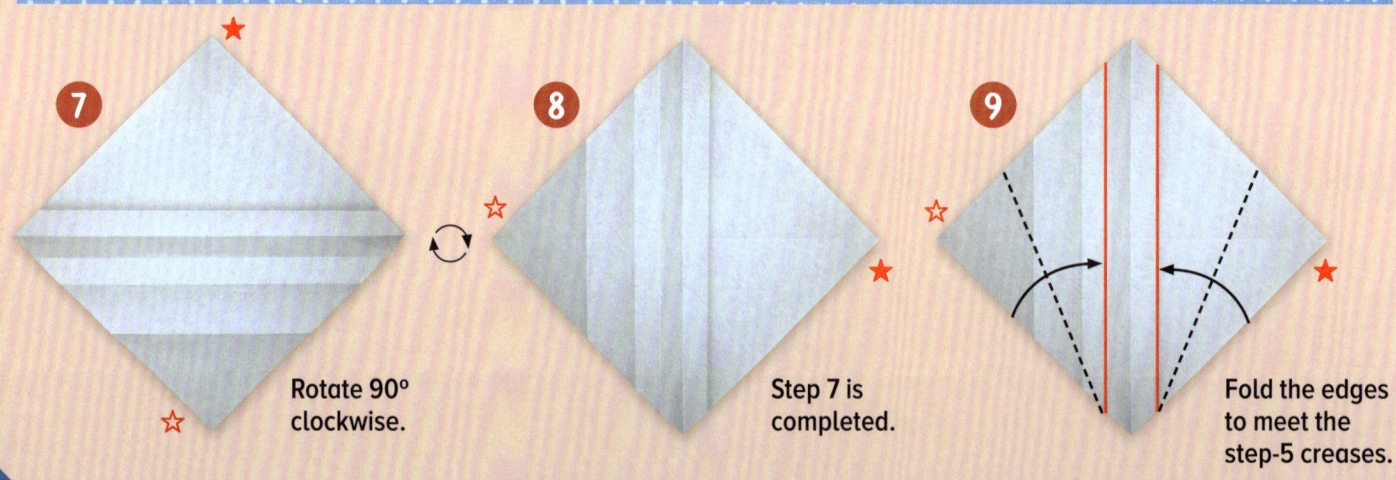

**7** Rotate 90° clockwise.

**8** Step 7 is completed.

**9** Fold the edges to meet the step-5 creases.

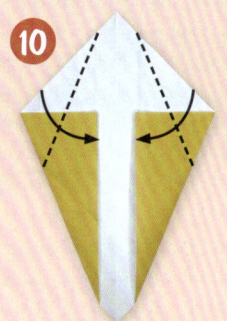
**10** Fold the top edges to meet the step-5 creases.

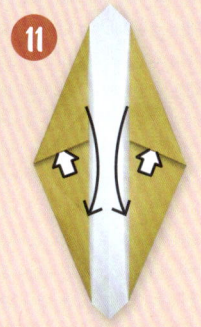
**11** Pull the hidden corners out, pivot them down, and squash them.

**12** Step 11 in progress.

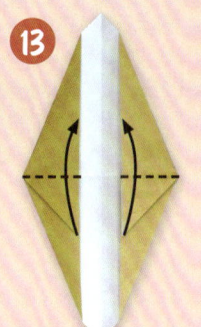
**13** Fold the flaps up.

**14** Step 13 is completed.

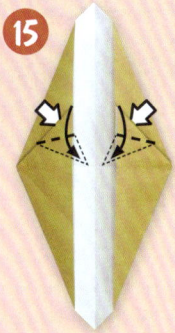
**15** Fold both flaps diagonally to meet the crease.

**16** Step 15 is completed. Flip it over left to right.

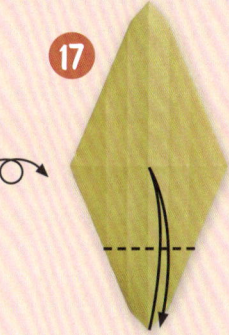
**17** Fold the bottom corner to the center. Unfold.

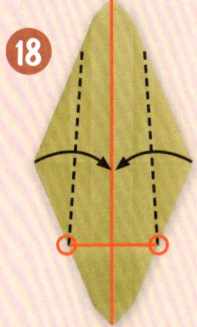
**18** Using the ○ positions as landmarks, fold the corners to the center.

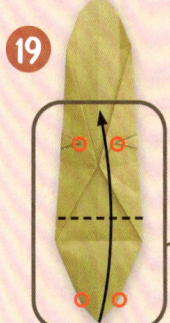
**19** Fold so that the paired ○ points meet.

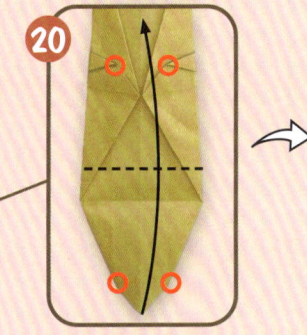
**20** Enlarged view of step 19.

**21** Fold along the ○-to-○ spans.

**22** Fold in a small portion of the bottom-right corner.

**23** Fold the left edge of the flap to align with the bottom edge.

**24** Fold in a small portion of the bottom-left corner.

**25** You can adjust the angle of flap ※ later to enable the model to stand. Flip it over.

**26** Fold so that the indicated ○ locations meet.

**27** Fold at the indicated position.

**28** Form the ear by step folding the corner.

**29** *Completed* Draw on the face. It's completed!

Mirror the angle of the crease in step 26 to change the direction the face is pointing.

▶ COOL AQUATIC & WATERSIDE ANIMALS

# Frog
▶ Photo on page 9

VIDEO:
tuttlepublishing.com/
unbelievably-cute-origami

We are perfect for spring decorations, and we can also be displayed standing up.

Large

Small

It can also stand up

- **Origami paper to use:** Head (Large): One 6-in (15-cm) sheet / Body (Large): One 6-in (15-cm) sheet; Head (Small): One 4¾-in (12-cm) sheet / Body (Small): One 4¾-in (12-cm) sheet
- **Recommended tools:** Black felt tip pen, round stickers (both large and small: ⅝ in / 1.5 cm), glue or masking tape

➡ The following instructions show 6-in (15-cm) origami paper being used.

## Head

**1** Fold corner to corner both ways. Unfold after each. (Back)

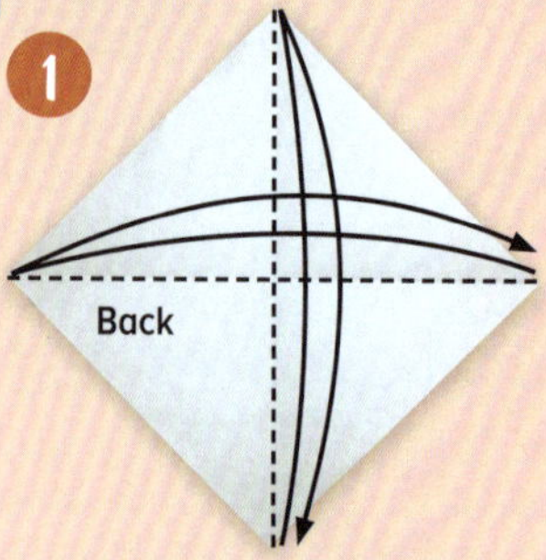

**2** Fold the corner to the center. Unfold.

**3** Fold the left edge to meet the step-2 crease.

**4** Fold the right edge to meet the step-2 crease.

**5** Fold down a small portion of the top corner. (Enlarged view of step 5.)

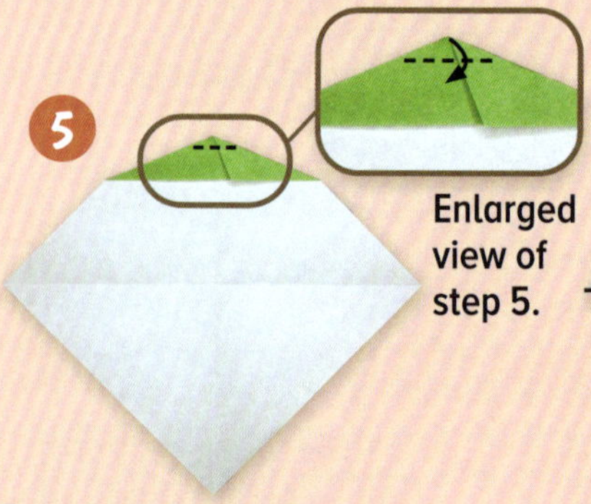

**6** Fold along the existing crease.

**7** Step 6 is completed. Flip it over.

**8** Fold the side corners to the bottom.

**9** Fold the flaps to the top. Unfold both.

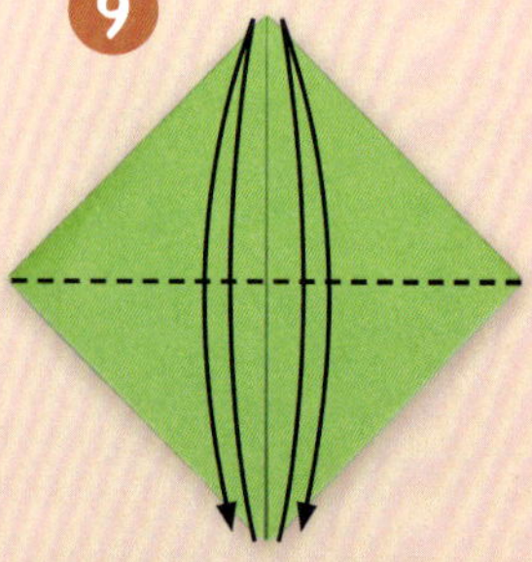

**10** Fold the flaps up diagonally as indicated. Approx. ⅜ in (1 cm)

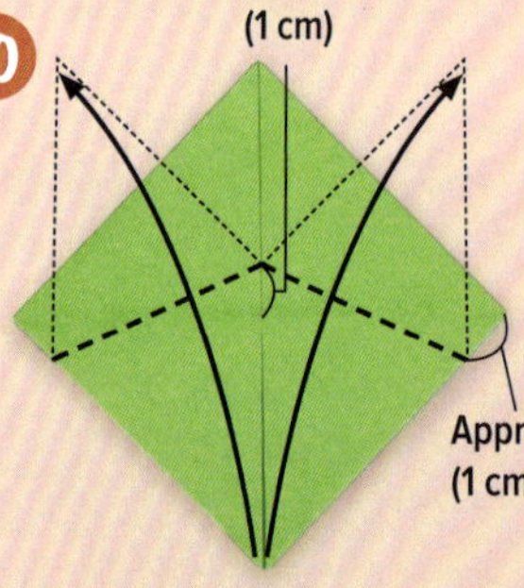

**11** Step 10 is completed.

**12** Fold down the tips of the flaps as indicated.

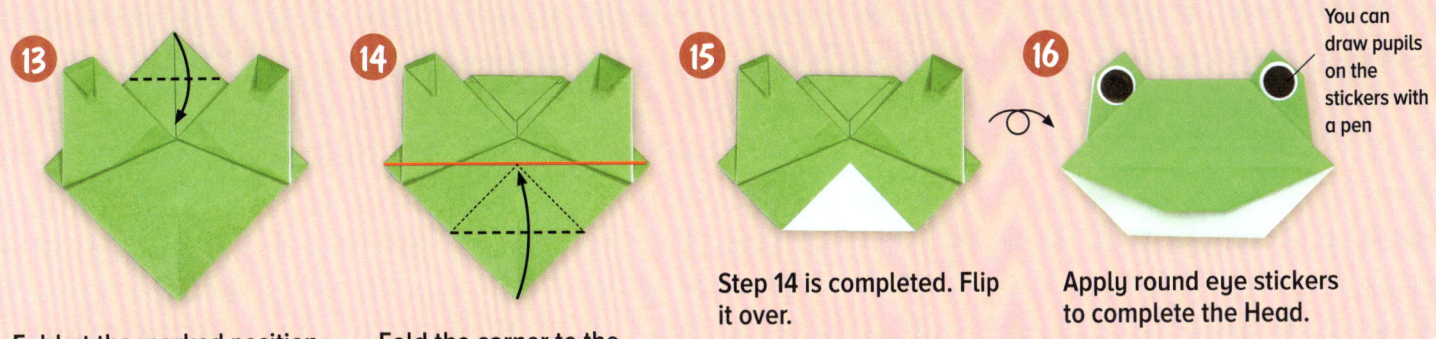

**13** Fold at the marked position.

**14** Fold the corner to the center.

**15** Step 14 is completed. Flip it over.

**16** Apply round eye stickers to complete the Head. You can draw pupils on the stickers with a pen

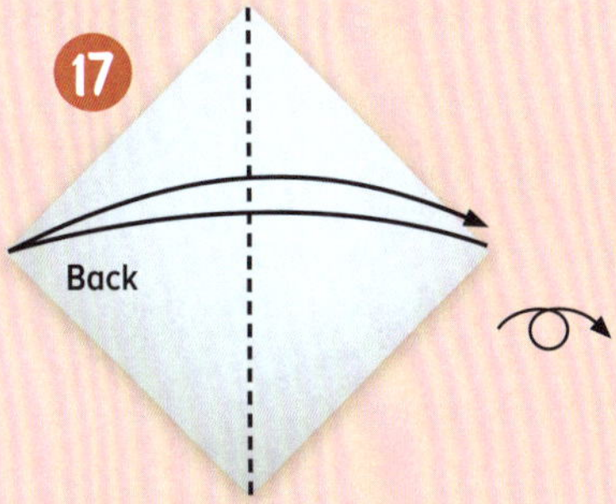

## Body

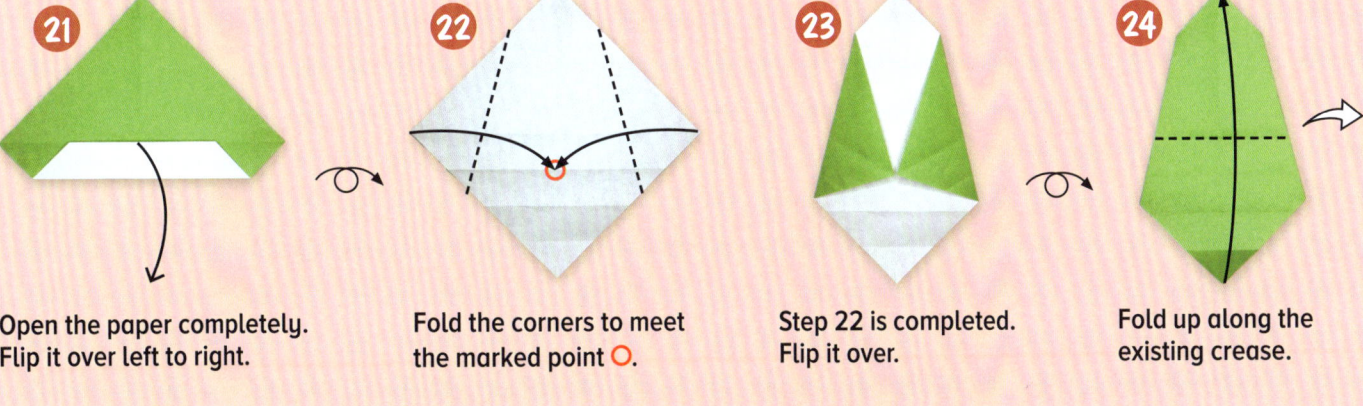

**17** Fold the paper in half corner to corner. Unfold. Flip it over.

**18** Fold the paper in half corner to corner. Unfold.

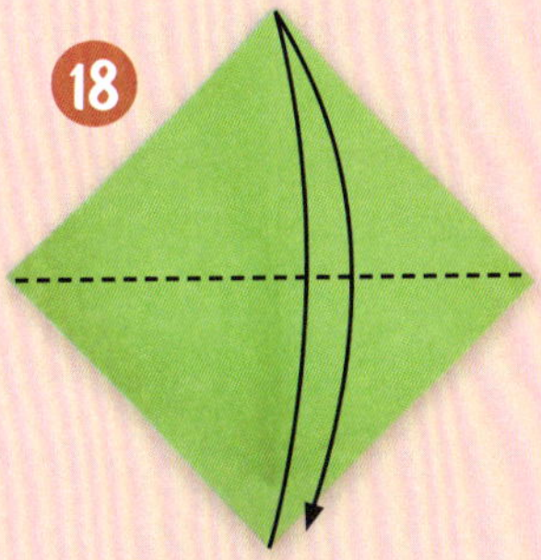

**19** Fold the corner to the center.

**20** Fold the edge to the center.

**21** Open the paper completely. Flip it over left to right.

**22** Fold the corners to meet the marked point ◯.

**23** Step 22 is completed. Flip it over.

**24** Fold up along the existing crease.

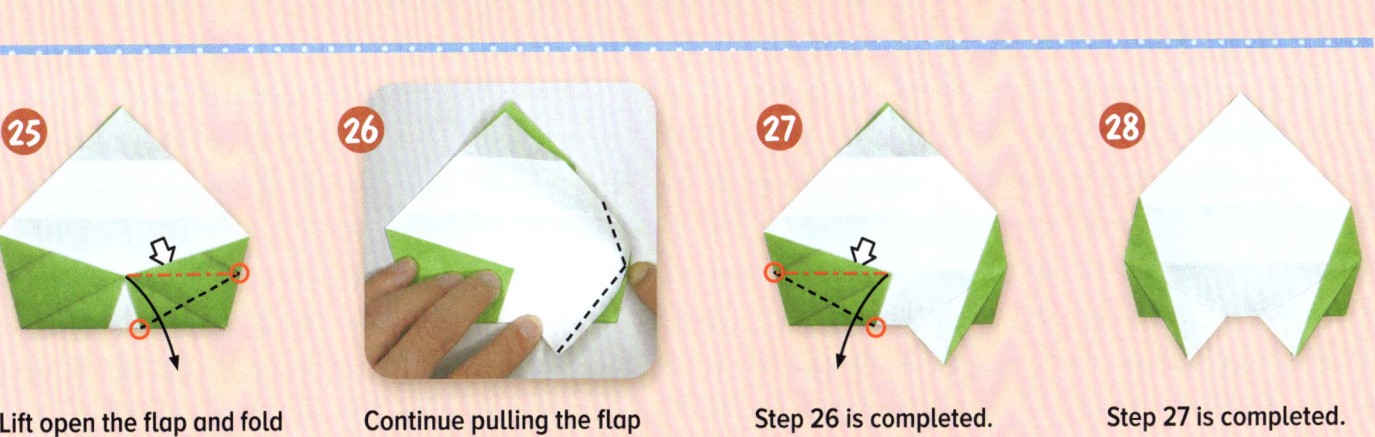

**25** Lift open the flap and fold along the ◯-to-◯ span.

**26** Continue pulling the flap down. Squash the pocket that forms on the right.

**27** Step 26 is completed. Mirror steps 25–26 on the left side.

**28** Step 27 is completed.

73

**29** Fold the indicated corners to meet the point ○ at the crease intersection.

**30** Step 29 is completed. Flip it over.

**31** Open the step-29 flap on the right.

**32** Fold along the ○-to-○ span. Unfold.

**33** Open the layer slightly, push the corner inward and fold down.

**34** While open, fold at the marked line and collapse.

**35** Mirror steps 31–34 on the left side.

**36** Step 35 is completed. Flip it over.

**37** Flip up the flaps at the bottom.

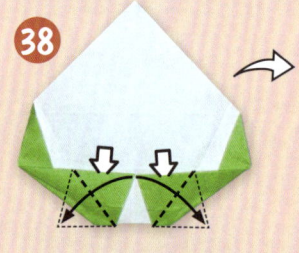
**38** Fold the corners out as indicated.

**39** Fold down the top corner of the uppermost layer along the existing crease.

**40** Fold down the flap along the existing crease.

**41** Fold along the ○-to-○ spans. Then, open the underlying pockets marked ※ and tuck the new flaps inside.

**42** Step 41 is completed.

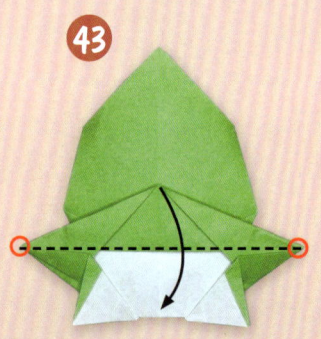
**43** Fold along the ○-to-○ span.

**44** Flip it over.

**45** The Body is completed! Adjust the angle of the flap from step 43 to enable the model to stand.

**Completed**
**46** Attach the Head to the Body with glue or tape to complete.

▶ ANIMAL MODELS FOR CELEBRATIONS

# Rabbit Dolls
▶ Photo on page 10

VIDEO: tuttlepublishing.com/unbelievably-cute-origami

We are a pair of cute rabbit dolls—male (*obina*) and female (*mebina*)—that you can decorate!

It can also stand up

- **Origami paper to use:** Female Doll (*Mebina*): One 6-in (15-cm) sheet / Fan (*Ougi*): One ¾-in (2-cm) sheet; Male Doll (*Obina*): One 6-in (15-cm) sheet / Scepter (*Shaku*): One ¾-in (2-cm) sheet
- **Recommended tools:** Black felt tip pen, glue, scissors

## Female Doll (*Mebina*)

**1**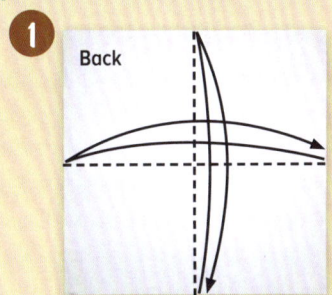
Fold edge to edge both ways. Unfold after each.

**2**
Fold the bottom edge to meet the center crease.

**3**
Approx. ⅜ in (1 cm)    Approx. ⅜ in (1 cm)
Fold in the bottom corners as indicated.

**4**
Fold equal segments of the bottom edge to the central vertical crease.

**5**
Approx. ⅜ in (1 cm)
Fold the bottom corner up as indicated.

**6**
While holding the left half of the uppermost flap ※ in place with a finger, pull out the underlying layer on the right.

**7**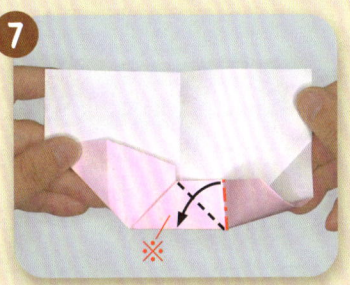
After pulling out the paper, recrease as indicated and flatten.

**8**
Step 7 is completed. Mirror steps 6–7 on the left side.

**9**
Step 8 is completed. Flip it over.

**10**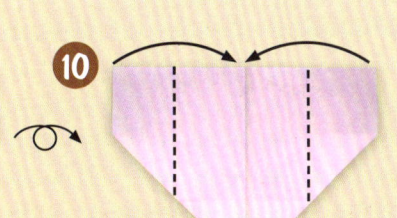
Fold both sides to the center.

**11**
Fold the top corners to the center. Unfold both.

**12**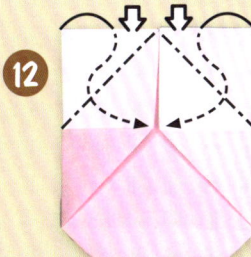
Inside reverse fold the corners along the step-11 creases.

**13**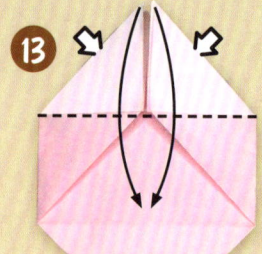

Fold down the uppermost flaps.

**14**

Fold the top corner to the crease. Unfold.

**15**

Fold the top corner to the step-14 crease.

**16**

Fold the top edge down to the step-14 crease.

**17**

Fold the top corners down to the step-14 crease.

**18**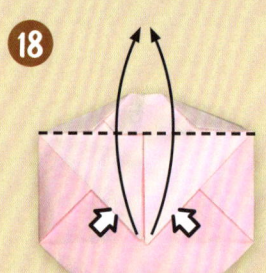

Swing the flaps back up.

**19**

Fold the outside edges in to the diagonal edges, bisecting the angles.

**20**

Fold both flaps corner to corner. Unfold both.

**21**

Enlarged view of step 20.

**22**

Inside reverse fold the corners along the creases from step 20.

**23**

Step 22 is completed.

**24**

Flip it over.

## Male Doll (Obina)

**25**

Fold small portions of the corners inside.

**26**

Draw on the face. The Female Doll is completed!

**24**

From the state at the beginning of step 24 of Mebina, fold the top flaps down diagonally.

**25**

Fold the flaps back up at angles slightly offset from those in the previous step.

**26** Fold in small portions of the corners.

**27** Step 26 is completed. Flip it over.

**28** Fold small portions of the indicated corners inside.

**29** Draw on the face. The Male Doll is completed!

## Scepter (*Shaku*)

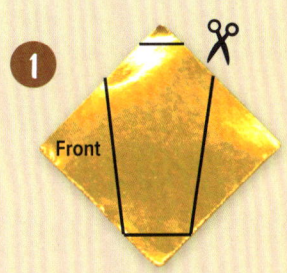

**1** Cut the paper as shown in the diagram.

**2** *Completed* — The Scepter is completed.

## Fan (*Ougi*)

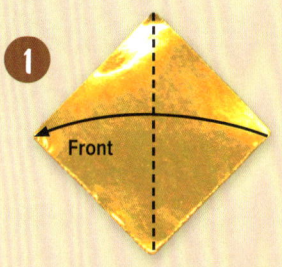

**1** Fold in half corner to corner.

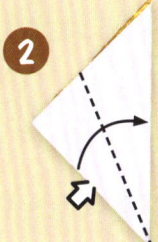

**2** Fold the uppermost layer edge to edge, bisecting the angle.

**3** Fold the lowermost layer behind along the edge of the step-2 flap.

**4** Cut through all layers as indicated.

**5** Open the paper completely.

**6** *Completed* — The Fan is completed.

---

*Completed* — Attach the Fan with a dab of glue to complete the *Mebina*.

*Completed* — Attach the Scepter with a dab of glue to complete the *Obina*.

Valley folding the indicated lowermost layers ※ enables the dolls to stand for display.

▶ ANIMAL MODELS FOR CELEBRATIONS

# Easter Bunny
▶ Photo on page 10

VIDEO:
tuttlepublishing.com/
unbelievably-cute-origami

With just a sheet of origami paper, you can make *me*—a sweet bunny peeping out from an eggshell!

It can also stand up

- **Origami paper to use:** One 6-in (15-cm) sheet
- **Recommended tools:** Black felt tip pen, markers

➔ If using patterned origami paper, start folding with the patterned side facing down so that the pattern appears on the eggshell portion.

**1**

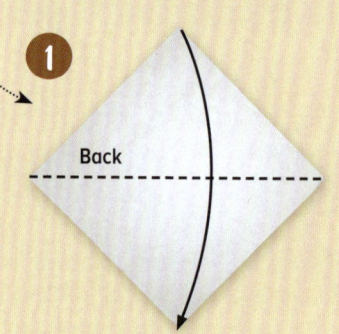

Fold the paper in half corner to corner.

**2**

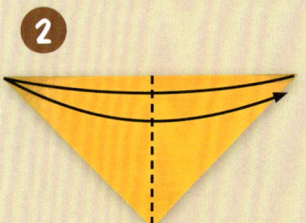

Fold corner to corner. Unfold.

**3**

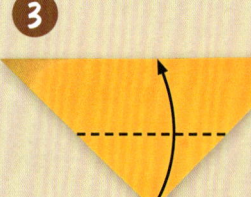

Fold both layers of the bottom corner up to meet the top edge.

**4**

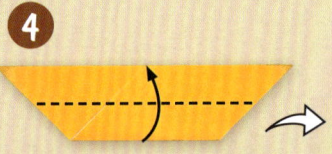

Fold the bottom edge up to meet the top edge.

**5**

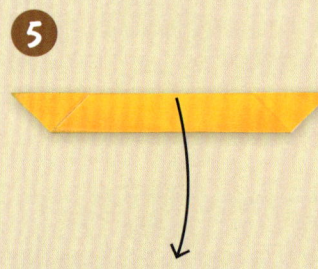

Open the paper to the state at step 2.

**6**

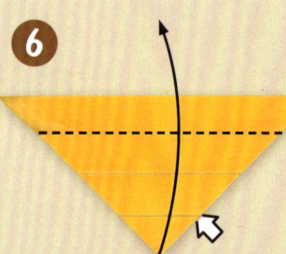

Fold the uppermost layer along the existing crease.

**7**

Fold the top corner to meet the edge of the flap. Unfold.

**8**

Fold so that the creases from steps 4 and 7 align.

**9**

Fold the corner up to meet the top edge.

**10**

Fold the flap edge up to the top edge.

**11**

Open the paper to the state at the beginning of step 9.

**12**

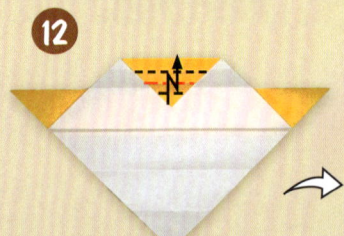

Step fold along the existing creases.

78

**13**

Step 12 is completed. Flip it over.

**14**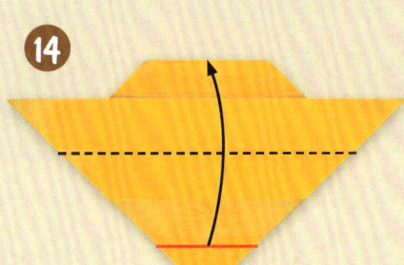

Fold the lowest crease up to meet the top edge.

**15**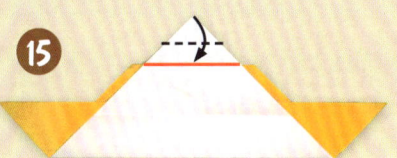

Fold the corner to the crease.

**16**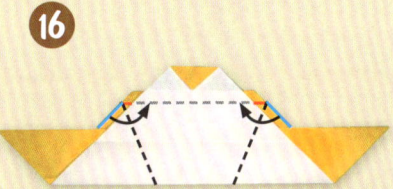

Fold the edges (—) to align with the underlying crease (----). Start on the right side.

**17**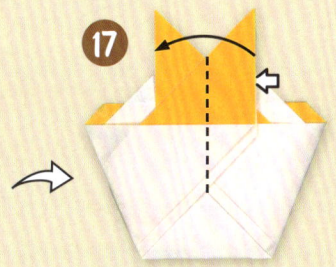

Fold the uppermost flap left at the center so that the free edge aligns with that of the underlying flap.

**18**

Pull out the underlying flap and reposition it to overlap the step-17 flap.

**19**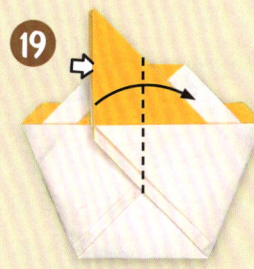

Fold the flap to the right in the center to mirror the underlying step-17 flap.

**20**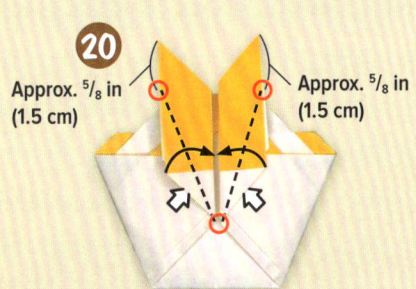

Approx. ⅝ in (1.5 cm)

Fold through all layers of the flaps along the ○-to-○ spans.

**21**

Open the layers of the flaps slightly and fold just the underlying layers diagonally.

**22**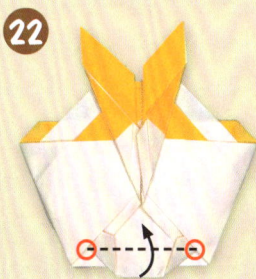

Fold along the ○-to-○ span.

**23**

Fold in small portions of the corners.

**24**

You can swing down the flap later to enable the model to stand.

**25**

Fold in the left and right corners to meet the adjacent creases.

**26**

To make a flat version, fold the edge of the step-22 flap to its base.

**27**

Swing the step-26 flap down. Flip it over.

**Completed**

**28**

Draw on the face. It's completed!

▶ ANIMAL MODELS FOR CELEBRATIONS

# Halloween Costumes
▶ Photo on page 11

VIDEO:
tuttlepublishing.com/
unbelievably-cute-origami

You can enjoy dressing us—and other animal models—in Halloween-style costumes!

- **Origami models to use:** Fox (Small)—see page 48; Tiger (Large)—see page 43
- **Origami paper to use for each character's accessories:** Hat: One 4-in (10-cm) sheet / Bow Tie: Two ¾-in (2-cm) sheets, Cape: One 3-in (7.5-cm) sheet
- **Recommended tools:** Glue, scissors

## Hat

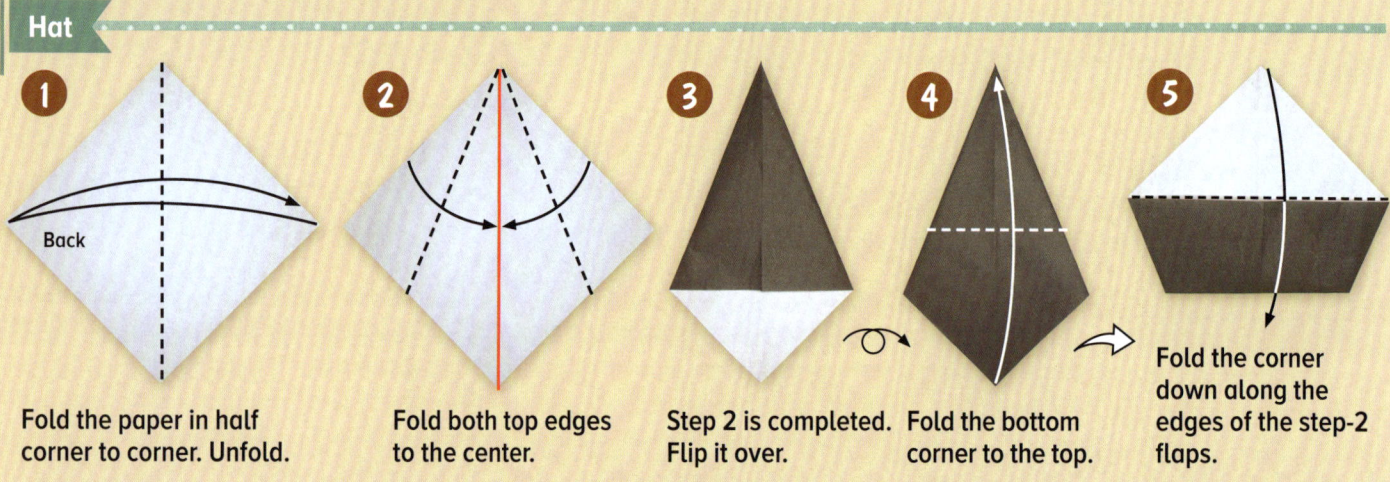

1. Fold the paper in half corner to corner. Unfold.
2. Fold both top edges to the center.
3. Step 2 is completed. Flip it over.
4. Fold the bottom corner to the top.
5. Fold the corner down along the edges of the step-2 flaps.

6. Fold the corner to the back side.
7. Open slightly and tuck the step-6 corner inside.
8. Fold the step-5 edge down to meet the bottom edge.
9. Fold the corners to the back side.
10. The Hat is completed.

## Bow Tie

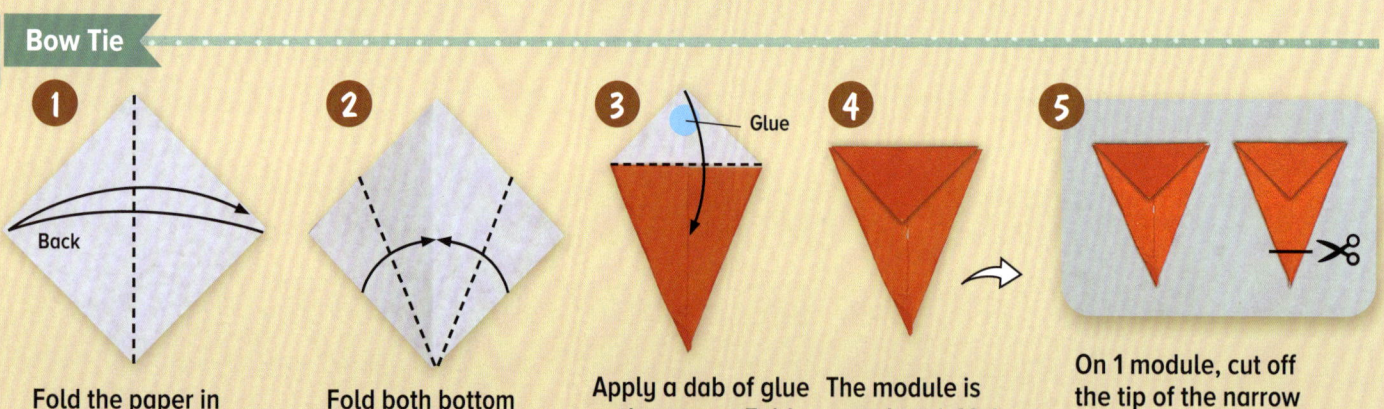

1. Fold the paper in half corner to corner. Unfold.
2. Fold both bottom edges to the center.
3. Apply a dab of glue to the corner. Fold along the edges of the step-2 flaps.
4. The module is completed. Make a second module just like this.
5. On 1 module, cut off the tip of the narrow corner.

## Cape for Fox (Small)

**6**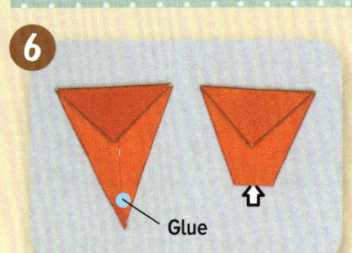
Apply a dab of glue to the narrow corner of the intact module and insert it into the pocket of the trimmed module.

**7**
Step 6 is completed. Flip it over.

**8**
The Bow Tie is completed.

**1**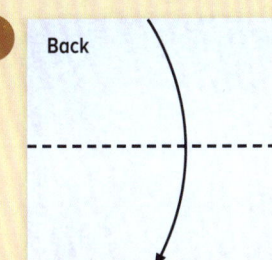
Back
Fold the paper in half edge to edge.

**2**
Step 1 is completed.

**3**
Prepare the Fox Body (page 49).

**4**
Fold the tail to the back.

**5**
Step 4 is completed.

**6**
Place the Body over the step-2 paper and fold at the indicated position.

## Cape for Tiger (Large)

**7**
Glue
Apply a dab of glue to the corner and fold the opposite side in mirror image to step 6.

**8**
The Cape is completed.

**9** *Completed*
Small Fox
Attach the Head, Bow Tie and Hat. It's completed!

**1**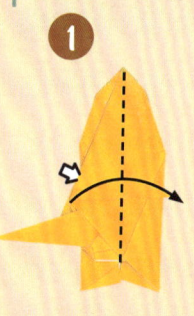
Prepare the Tiger Body (pages 44–45). Flip it over. Flip 1 layer to the right.

**2**
Swing the flap down along the existing diagonal crease.

**3**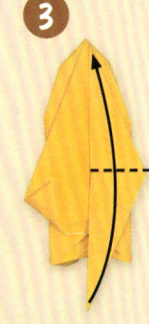
Swing the flap up along the horizontal crease.

**4**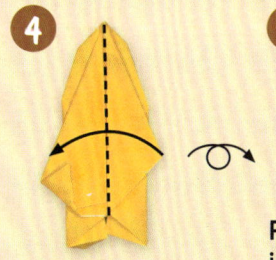
Flip 1 layer to the left. Flip it over.

**5**
Prepare the Cape paper in the same manner as for the Fox (see above).

**6**
Glue
Place the Body over the Cape paper and fold at the indicated positions.

**7**
The Cape is completed.

**8** *Completed*
Large Tiger
Attach the Head, Bow Tie and Hat. It's completed!

## ▶ ANIMAL MODELS FOR CELEBRATIONS

# Chimney Cat
▶ Photo on page 11

VIDEO: tuttlepublishing.com/ unbelievably-cute-origami

Draw in my face and the chimney's mortar pattern with a pen.

Attach a string to turn it into a Christmas ornament!

- ▶ **Origami paper to use:** One 6-in (15-cm) sheet
- ▶ **Recommended tools:** Black felt tip pen, markers, white paint pen

**1**

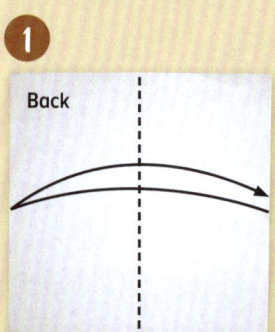

Fold the paper in half edge to edge. Unfold.

**2**

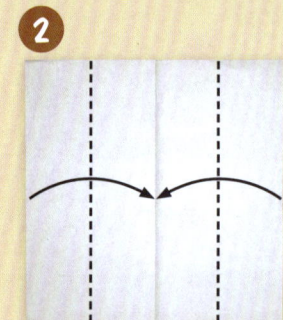

Fold the edges to align with the crease.

**3**

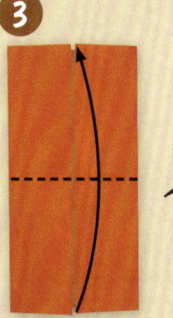

Fold the bottom edge to the top edge.

**4**

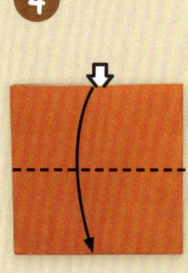

Fold the top edge of the uppermost flap down to the bottom edge.

**5**

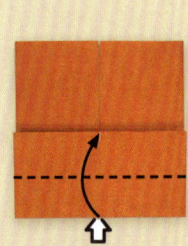

Fold the bottom edge of the uppermost flap up to the folded edge.

**6**

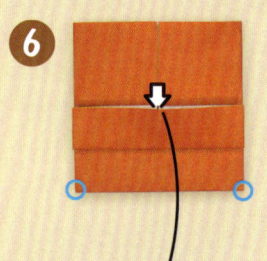

Without altering the step-4 and step-5 folds, swing the paper open along the ○-to-○ span.

**7**

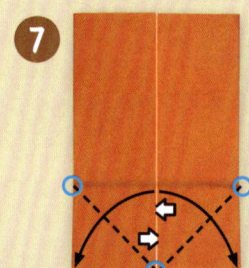

Open the paper while folding along the ○-to-○ spans to spread it out.

**8**

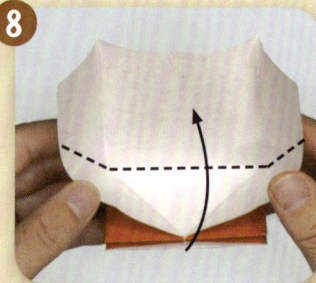

Fold the bottom portion up along the crease. The sides will flatten with diagonal creases.

**9**

Step 8 in progress.

**10**

Step 8 is completed. Flip it over.

**11**

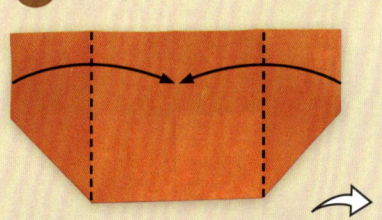

Fold the edges in to meet the center.

**12**

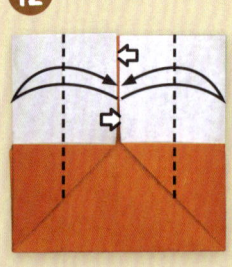

Fold the flap edges to the outside edges. Return them to the center.

**13**

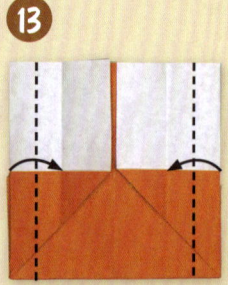

Fold the 2 uppermost layers of the outside edges to the step-12 creases.

**14**
Flatten the pocket (※) that opens up on each side into a triangle.

**15**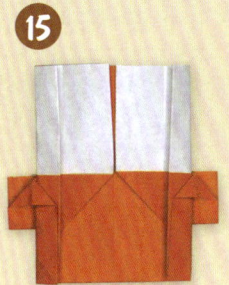
Steps 13 and 14 are completed.

**16**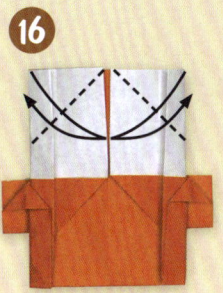
Fold the top corners to the center. Unfold both.

**17**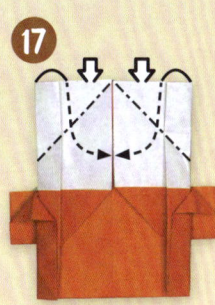
Inside reverse fold the corners.

**18**
Step 17 is completed.

**19**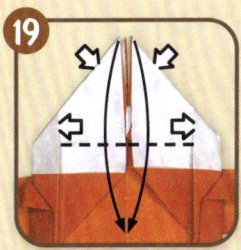
Open the flanking strips a little and swing the 2 triangular flaps down.

**20**
Fold the corner to the crease.

**21**
Fold the step-19 flaps up diagonally to align with the edges of the step-20 flap.

**22**
Open the flanking strips a little and fold the small corners up.

**23**
Step 22 is completed. Flip it over.

**24**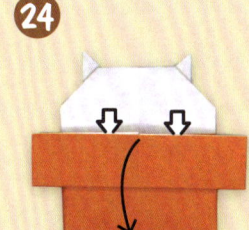
Swing the uppermost flap down.

**25**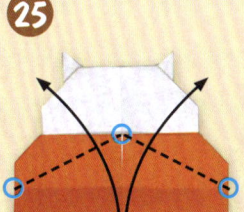
Open while folding along the ○-to-○ spans.

**26**
Swing the horizontal edge up and squash the outside corners as you flatten the paper.

**27**
Fold the outside corners behind along the existing creases.

**28**
Fold the flaps down along the horizontal edge.

**29**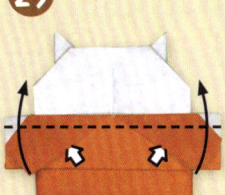
Fold the flaps back up at the indicated position.

**30**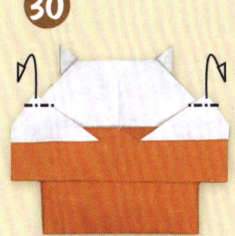
Fold small portions of the flap corners to the back.

**31**
Tuck the overlapping sections ⌐ ⌐ inside the underlying pocket.

**Completed**

**32**
Draw on the face and mortar pattern to complete!

83

▶ ANIMAL MODELS FOR CELEBRATIONS

# Santa's-Boot Cat
▶ Photo on page 11

VIDEO:
tuttlepublishing.com/
unbelievably-cute-origami

If you attach a string to my back, I can also be used as a Christmas ornament!

- **Origami paper to use:** Half of one 6-in (15-cm) sheet (6 × 3 in / 15 × 7.5 cm)
- **Recommended tools:** Black felt tip pen, markers, glue

**1** 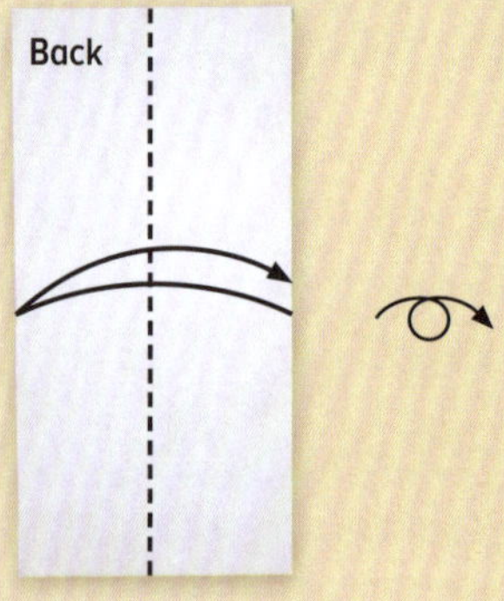 Fold the paper in half edge to edge. Unfold. Flip it over.

**2** 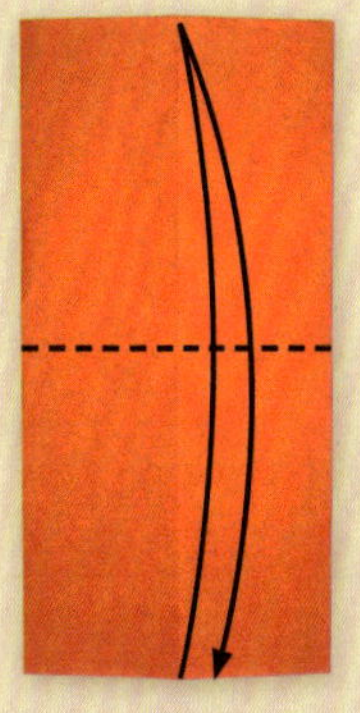 Fold the bottom edge to the top edge. Unfold.

**3** 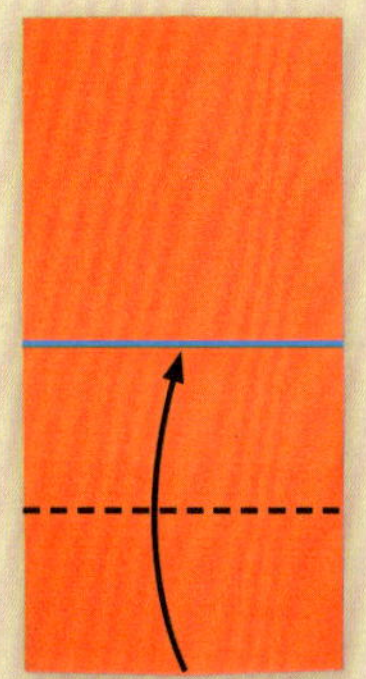 Fold the bottom edge to the horizontal crease.

**4** 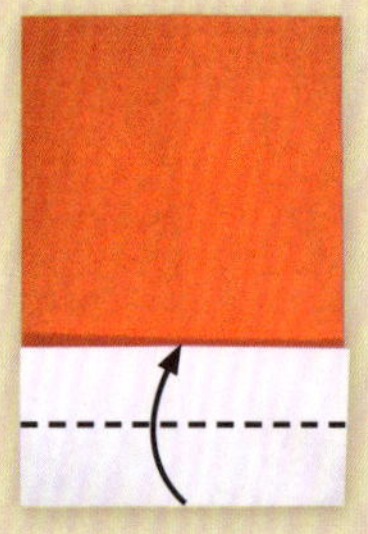 Fold the bottom folded edge up to meet the step-2 edge.

**5** 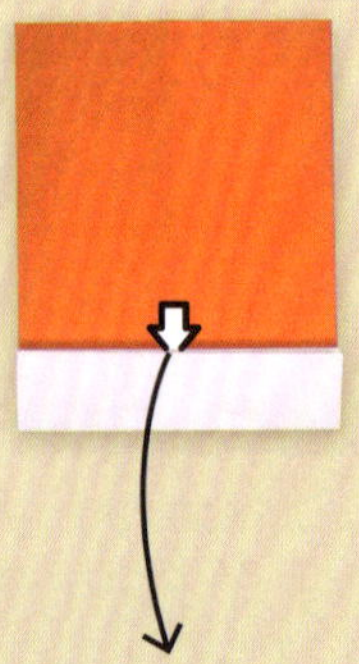 Return the paper to the state at step 2.

**6** 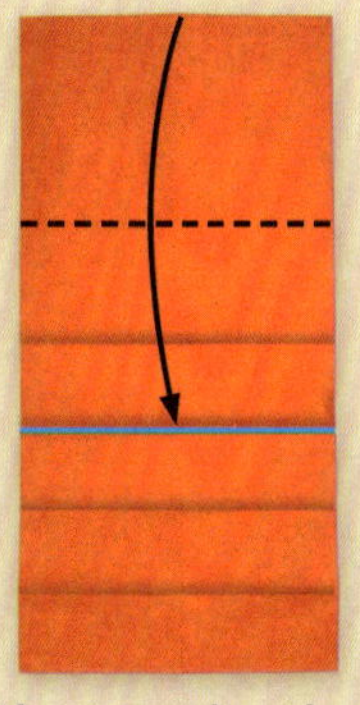 Fold the top edge down to meet the third crease from the bottom.

**7** 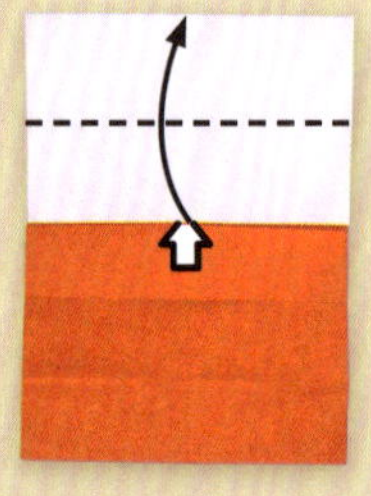 Fold the flap edge up to meet the top folded edge.

**8** 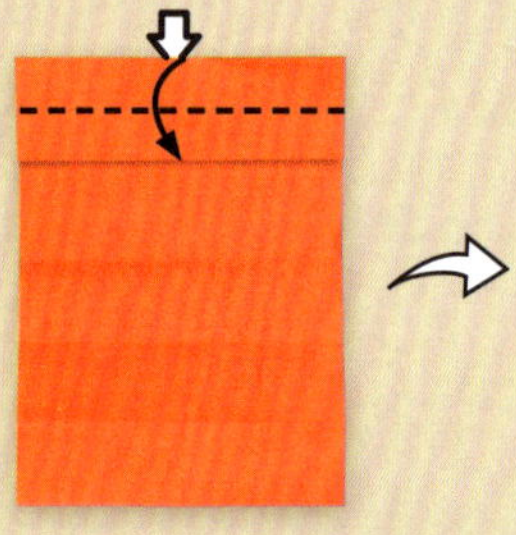 Fold the uppermost layer's edge down to meet the folded edge.

**9** 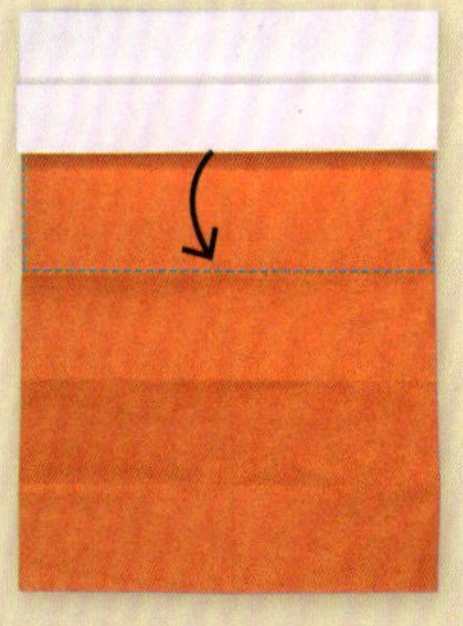 Return the paper to the state at the beginning of step 7.

**10** 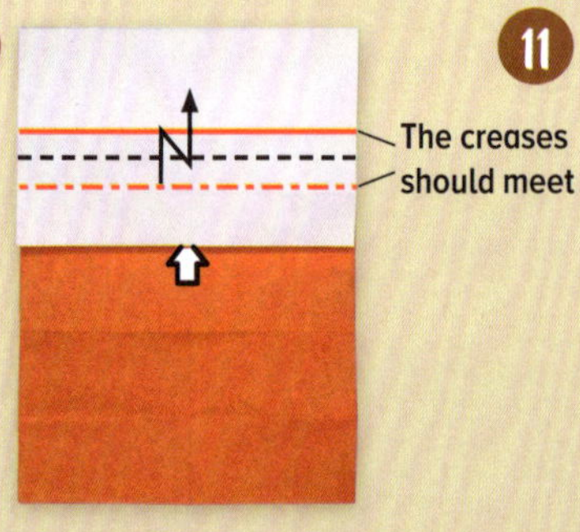 Step fold so that the step-8 crease meets the step-7 crease. The creases should meet

**11**  Step 10 is completed. Flip it over.

**12** 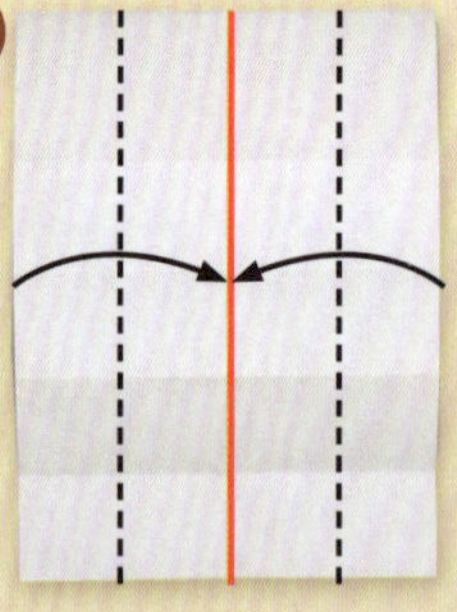 Fold both side edges in to the center.

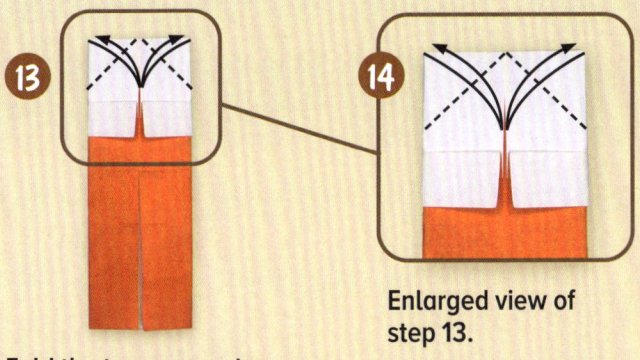
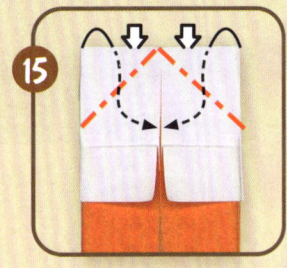

**13** Fold the top corners to the center. Unfold both.

**14** Enlarged view of step 13.

**15** Inside reverse fold the corners.

**16** Swing the 2 triangular flaps down.

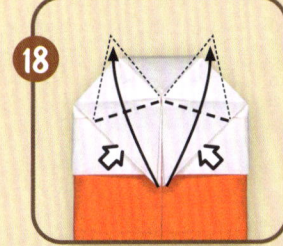

**17** Fold the corner to the crease.

**18** Fold the step-16 flaps up diagonally to align with the edges of the step-17 flap.

**19** Step 18 is completed. Flip it over.

**20** Step 19 is completed.

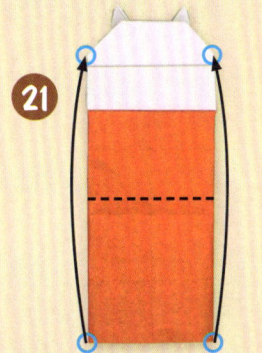

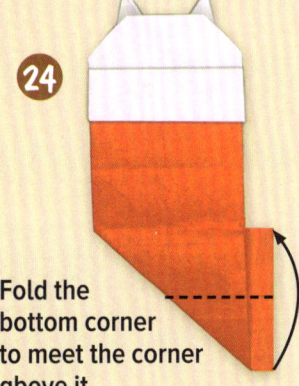

**21** Fold so that the paired points meet.

**22** Fold the uppermost layer so that the 2 edges meet.

**23** Swing the uppermost flap down.

**24** Fold the bottom corner to meet the corner above it

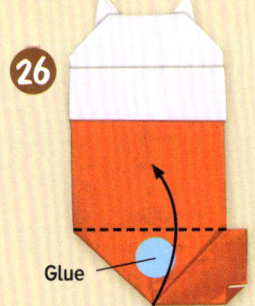

**25** Fold in a small portion of the bottom-right corner.

**26** Glue. Apply a dab glue to the indicated location, then fold the flap up along the existing crease.

**Completed**

**27** Draw on the face and color in the coat markings. Completed.

85

▶ ANIMAL MODELS FOR CELEBRATIONS

# Reindeer
▶ Photo on page 11

VIDEO:
tuttlepublishing.com/
unbelievably-cute-origami

My most striking features are my large, pointy antlers, made with step folds.

▶ **Origami paper to use:** One 6-in (15-cm) sheet
▶ **Recommended tools:** Black felt tip pen, round sticker (red, 3/16 in / 5 mm)

**1**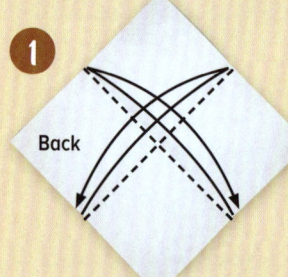
Fold edge to edge both ways. Unfold after each.

**2**
Fold the bottom edges to meet the step-1 creases. Unfold after each.

**3**
Fold the top edges to meet the step-2 creases. Unfold after each.

**4**
Step 3 is completed. Flip it over left to right.

**5**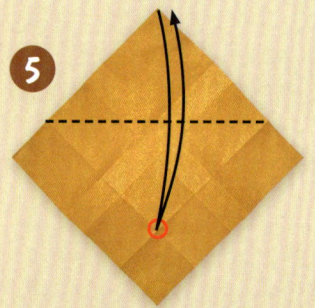
Fold the top corner to the ○ mark. Unfold.

**6**
Step 5 is completed. Flip it over left to right.

**7**
Fold the top corner to the ○ mark.

**8**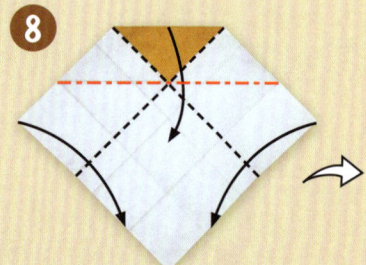
Collapse the paper along the creases.

**9**
Step 8 in progress.

**10**
Step 8 is completed. Flip it over left to right.

**11**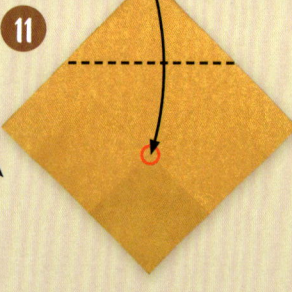
Fold the top corner to the ○ mark.

**12**
Step 11 is completed. Flip it over.

**13**
Partially open the right flap.

**14**
Pivot to shift the layers as indicated, then squash.

**15**
Steps 13 and 14 are completed.

**16**
Fold the corner to meet the edge.

**17**
Step 16 is completed. Mirror steps 13–16 on the left flap.

**18**
Step 17 is completed.

**19**
Flip 1 layer to the left and fold.

**20**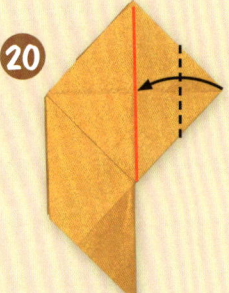
Fold the corner to the intersection of creases.

**21**
Fold the corner out so that it protrudes slightly beyond the underlying edge.

**22**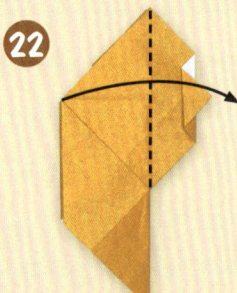
Flip 2 layers to the right.

**23**
Fold the corner to the intersection of creases.

**24**
Fold the corner out so that it protrudes slightly beyond the underlying edge.

**25**
Flip 1 layer to the left.

**26**
Fold the edges to align with the center.

**27**
Fold the corners diagonally along the folded edges.

**28**
Fold the flaps edge to edge, bisecting the angles.

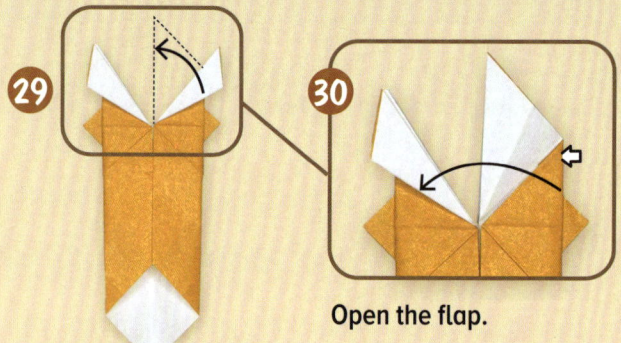

29 Unfold the flap on the right to its step-27 state.

30 Open the flap.

31 Refold along the creases as indicated.

32 Step 31 is completed. Mirror steps 29–31 on the left side.

33 Step 32 is completed. Flip it over.

34 Fold the corner inside.

35 Fold along the ○-to-○ span.

36 Fold the bottom corners to the center. Flip it over.

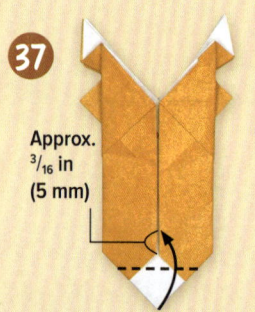

37 Approx. 3/16 in (5 mm)
Fold the corner up as indicated.

38 Step 37 is completed. Flip it over.

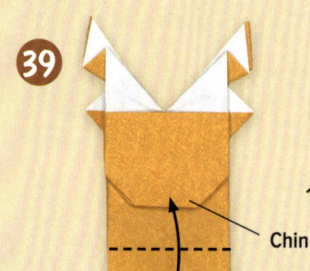

39 Chin
Fold so that the bottom edge slightly overlaps the chin.

40 Tuck the overlapped part underneath.

41 Step 40 is completed. Flip it over.

42 Fold the bottom corners in diagonally.

43 Step 42 is completed. Flip it over.

44 **Completed**
Apply a red round sticker for the nose and draw on the eyes. Completed.

▶ ANIMAL MODELS FOR CELEBRATIONS

# Full-Moon Rabbit
▶ Photo on page 11

VIDEO: tuttlepublishing.com/unbelievably-cute-origami

My face is set against the backdrop of a full moon. How cool is that?

- **Origami paper to use:** One 6-in (15-cm) sheet
- **Recommended tools:** Black felt tip pen, markers

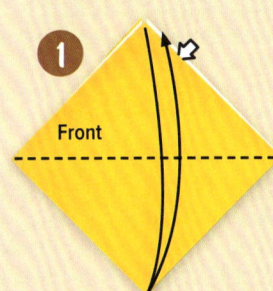

**1** Begin with a Square Base (page 14). Rotate it so that the open side faces up. Fold the top corner of the uppermost layer to the bottom. Unfold.

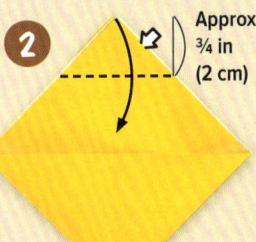

**2** Fold the top corner of the uppermost layer at the indicated position.

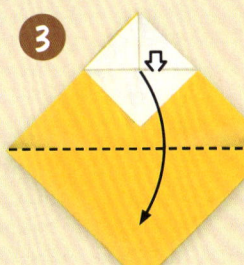

**3** Swing the flap down along the existing crease.

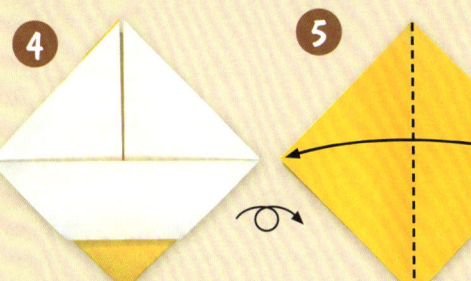

**4** Step 3 is completed. Flip it over left to right.

**5** Flip 1 flap to the left.

**6** Fold the edge to the center.

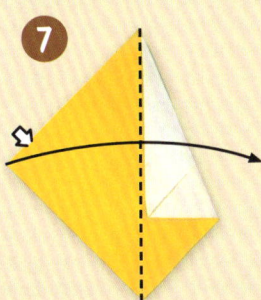

**7** Flip 2 flaps to the right.

**8** Fold the edge to the center.

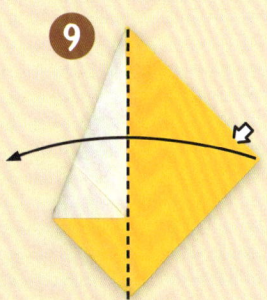

**9** Flip 1 flap to the left.

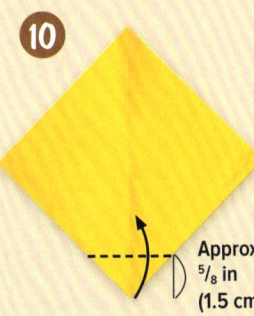

**10** Fold the bottom corner up at the indicated position.

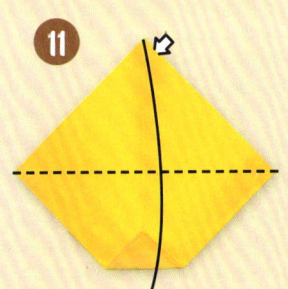

**11** Fold the uppermost layer at the indicated position.

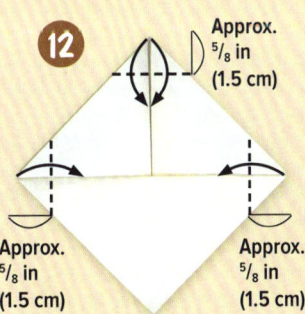

**12** Fold in 4 flaps at the indicated positions.

**13** Step 12 is completed. Flip it over.

**14** Fold the corner up at the folded edge and tuck it inside.

**Completed**

**15** Draw on the face, and it's completed!

▶ Practical Animal Origami Models

# Rabbit Chopstick Holder
▶ Photo on page 12

VIDEO: tuttlepublishing.com/unbelievably-cute-origami

Cute chopstick sleeves are sure to be a hit at parties and more!

- ▶ **Origami paper to use:** One 6-in (15-cm) sheet
- ▶ **Recommended tools:** Black felt tip pen, markers, glue

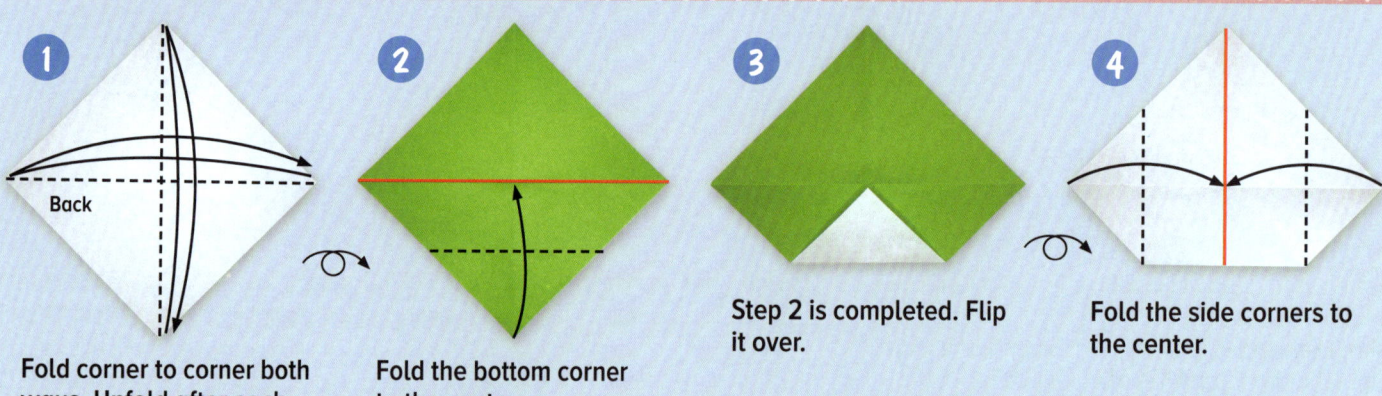

**1** Fold corner to corner both ways. Unfold after each. Flip it over.

**2** Fold the bottom corner to the center.

**3** Step 2 is completed. Flip it over.

**4** Fold the side corners to the center.

**5** Fold the corners to the outside folded edges.

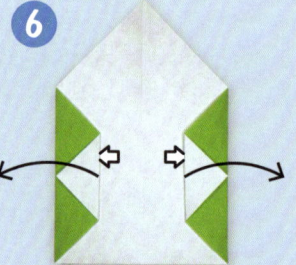
**6** Swing open the left and right flaps.

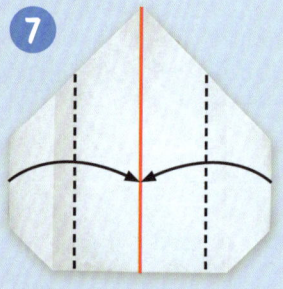
**7** Fold the outside folded edges to the center.

**8** Open the flap to the left.

**9** Fold the outside folded edge to the center.

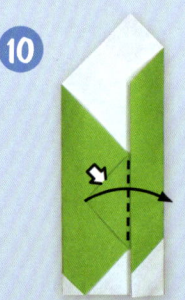
**10** Flip 2 flaps to the right.

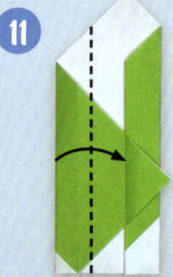
**11** Fold the outside folded edge to the center.

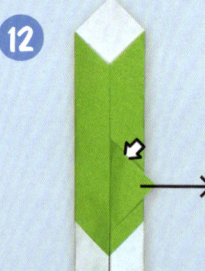
**12** Pull out the uppermost flap corner to the right.

### 13
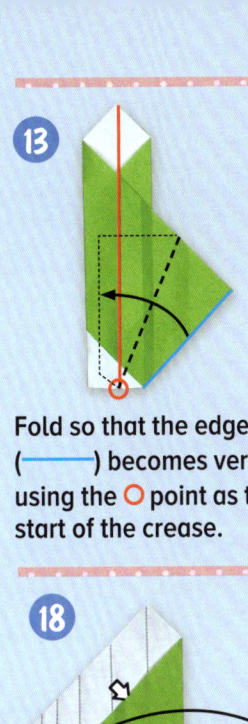
Fold so that the edge (———) becomes vertical, using the ○ point as the start of the crease.

### 14
Open the corner to the left.

### 15
Flip the flap to the left.

### 16
Pull out the corner to the left.

### 17
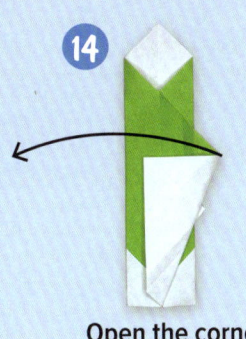
Fold so that the edge (———) becomes vertical, using the ○ point as the start of the crease.

### 18
Open the corner to the right.

### 19

Fold the corners in along the outermost creases.

### 20
Fold in along the first crease to the right of the center.

### 21
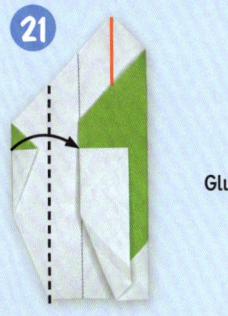
Fold in through both layers along the second crease to the left of the center.

### 22
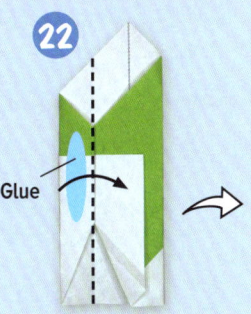
Apply glue in the indicated location and fold the flap in along the existing crease.

### 23
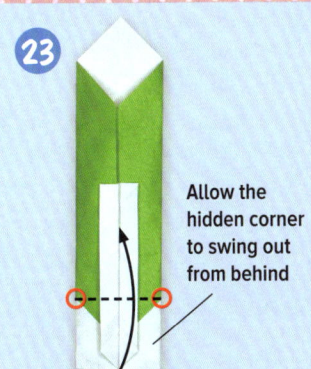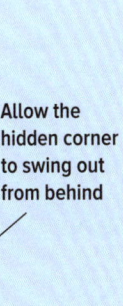
Allow the hidden corner to swing out from behind
Fold along the ○-to-○ span.

### 24
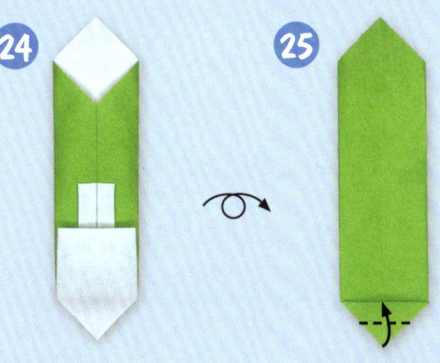
Step 23 is completed. Flip it over.

### 25
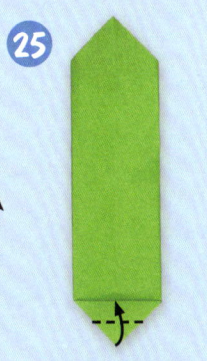
Fold the corner up to the folded edge.

### 26

Step 25 is completed. Flip it over.

### 27
Step 26 is completed.

### 28
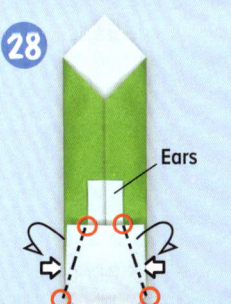
Ears
Fold the corners behind the ears along the ○-to-○ spans.

### 29

Fold small portions of the corners behind.

### Completed
### 30

Draw on the face, and it's completed!

**91**

# Practical Animal Origami Models

## Cat Bookmark
▶ Photo on page 13

I'll hold your page, and look adorable while doing it! I make a great gift, too.

VIDEO: tuttlepublishing.com/unbelievably-cute-origami

Tiger Cat Version

Calico Cat Version

▶ **Origami paper to use:** One 6-in (15-cm) sheet
▶ **Recommended tools:** Black felt tip pen, white paint pen, markers, round stickers (black, 3/16 in / 5 mm)

→ If you start with the white side of the origami paper facing up, you can make the calico cat version.

**Method to make legs of equal length begins at step 24**

**1**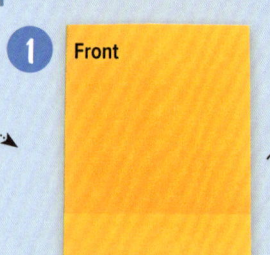
Start from step 14 of Relaxed Cat (page 24). Turn the paper over.

**2**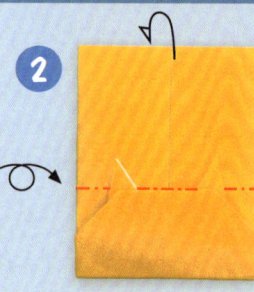
Make a mountain fold at the indicated position.

**3**
Step 2 is completed. Flip it over.

**4**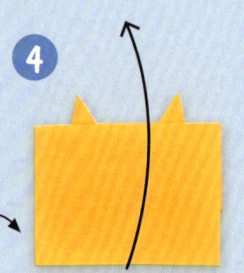
Swing the bottom edge up.

**5**
Rotate 180°.

**6**
Fold the top corners to the crease. Unfold both.

**7**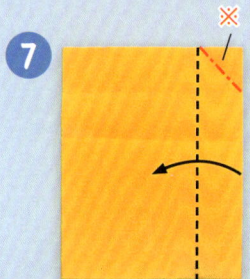
Fold the right edge to the center. At the same time, squash the point marked ✻ into a triangle.

**8**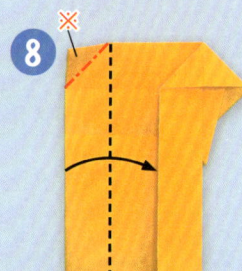
Mirror step 7 on the left side.

**9**
Step 8 is completed.

**10**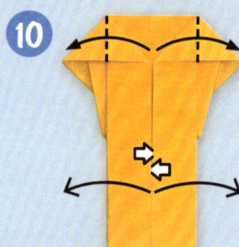
Open the flaps to sides, folding the triangles at the top in half.

**11**
Fold only in the specified locations.

**12**
Mountain fold at the indicated location. Then, return the paper to the state in step 11.

**13**
Swing the paper up from behind at the top. Look ahead to step 14 for the shape.

**14**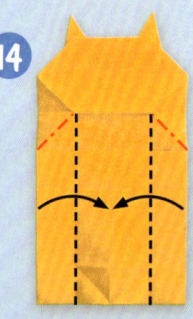
Collapse the paper along the existing creases

**15**
Step 14 is completed. Flip it over.

**16**
Open the flaps to the left and right.

**17**
Fold along the indicated creases, opening a pocket. Squash it into a diamond shape.

**18**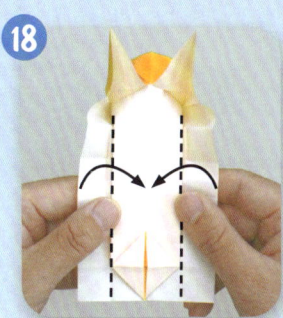
While opening the back side, close the left and right sides in front.

**19**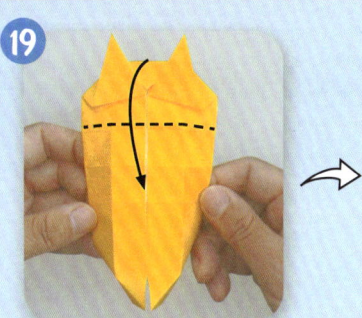
Fold along the crease.

**20**
Step 19 is completed. Flip it over.

**21**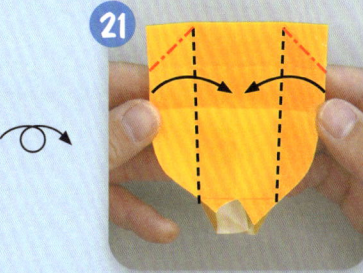
Fold the sides to the center along the existing creases. Squash the structures at the top into triangles.

**22**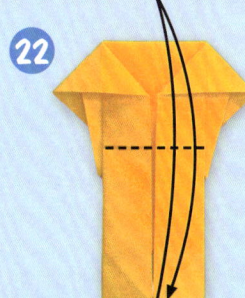
Reverse the existing crease and press firmly. Unfold.

**23**
Fold the flap up at the indicated position.

**24**
Step 23 is completed. Flip the paper over and rotate it 180°.

**25**
Fold small portions of the 4 indicated corners behind.

**Completed**
**26**
Draw on the face and color in the coat markings to complete.

Use a pen or apply round stickers

### Variation: Make different leg lengths

**24**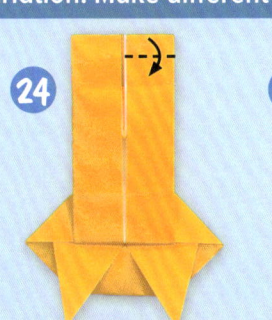
To make the leg lengths different, begin with the paper folded to the state of the beginning of step 24. Fold down a small portion of 1 leg.

**25**
Open the paper at the ★ position.

**26**
Fold down along the crease.

**27**
Close up the part that was opened.

**28**
Fold in small portions of the 4 indicated corners. Flip the paper over and rotate it 180°.

**Completed**
**29**
Draw on the face and color in the coat markings to complete.

Insert it into a book as if tucking the page under the cat's chin.

▶ Practical Animal Origami Models

# Cat (or Bear) Envelope
▶ Photo on page 12

VIDEO:
tuttlepublishing.com/
unbelievably-cute-origami

If you change the shape of my ears, I become a Bear Envelope!
➜ page 96

- **Origami paper to use:** One 6-in (15-cm) sheet
- **Recommended tools:** black felt tip pen, markers, sticker

**1**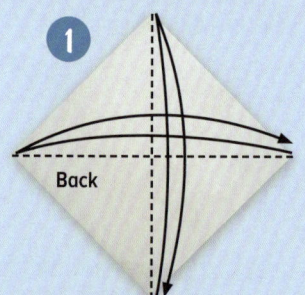
Fold corner to corner both ways. Unfold after each.

**2**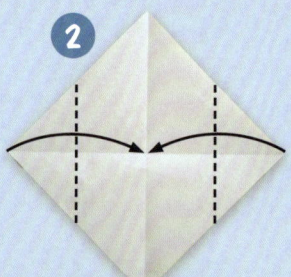
Fold the side corners to the center.

**3**
Step 2 is completed. Turn the paper over.

**4**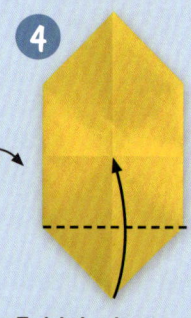
Fold the bottom corner to the center.

**5**
Step 4 is completed. Turn the paper over.

**6**
Fold the side edges to the center.

**7**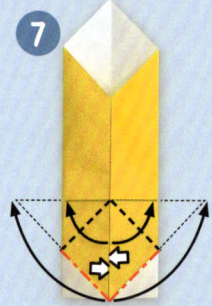
Open up the flaps and fold the bottom inside corners to the outside.

**8**
Step 7 in progress. Allow the triangular corner to swing forward from behind.

**9**
Step 7 is completed.

**10**
Fold the diagonal edges in to align with the vertical edges.

**11**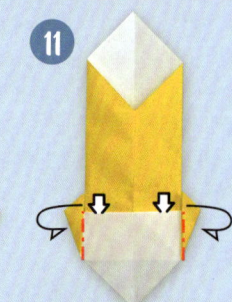
Open up pockets and fold the corners inside.

**12**
Approx. ¾ in (2 cm)
Mountain fold 3 corners to the inside at the indicated positions.

**13**
Step 12 is completed.

**14**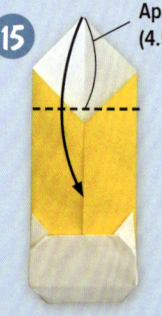
Insert note, folded money or similar items inside.

**15**
Approx. 1¾ in (4.5 cm)
Fold at the indicated position.

**16**
Seal with a sticker.

**17**
Completed
Draw on the face and markings. The Cat Envelope is completed.

94

▶ Practical Animal Origami Models

# Cat (or Bear) Message Card
▶ Photo on page 13

VIDEO:
tuttlepublishing.com/
unbelievably-cute-origami

If you change the shape of my ears, I become a Bear Message Card!
➡ page 96

- ▶ **Origami paper to use:** One 6-in (15-cm) sheet
- ▶ **Recommended tools:** black felt tip pen, markers

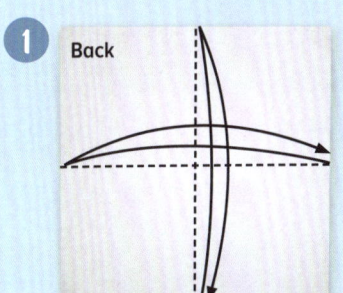

**1** Fold edge to edge both ways. Unfold after each.

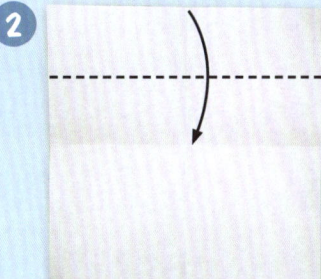

**2** Fold the top edge to meet the center crease.

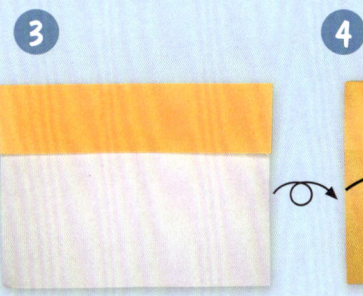

**3** Step 2 is completed. Turn the paper over left to right.

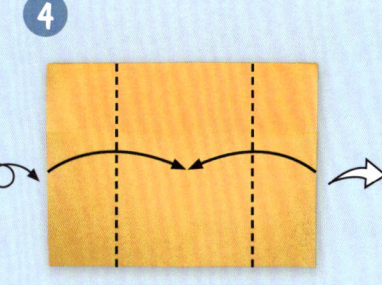

**4** Fold the side edges to the center.

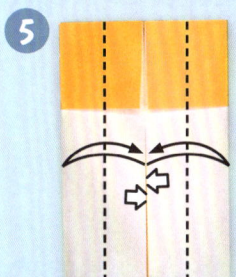

**5** Fold the free edges in the center to the outside folded edges. Unfold both.

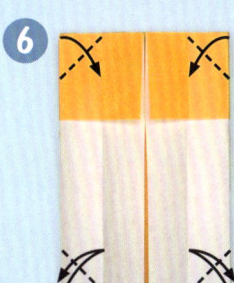

**6** Fold all 4 outside corners to the step-5 creases. Unfold the bottom 2 corners.

**7** Inside reverse fold the bottom 2 corners.

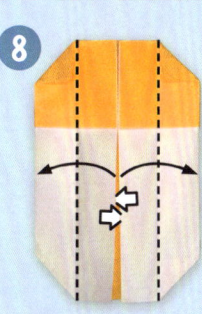

**8** Fold along the existing creases.

**9** Step 8 is completed. Turn the paper over.

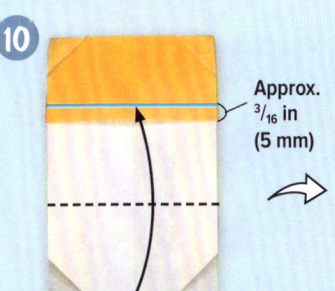

**10** Fold the bottom edge to the indicated position.

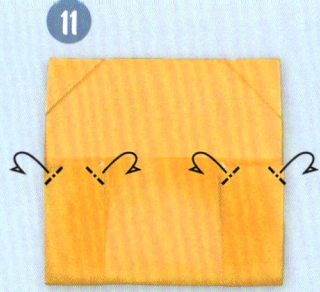

**11** Fold small portions of the 4 indicated corners behind.

**12** Insert the overlapping section ★ into the underlying pocket.

**13** Completed

Draw on the face, paw pads and fur markings. The Cat Message Card is completed.

## Write a message on the Cat (or Bear) Message Card

14 Open the ※ section.

15 Step 14 is completed.

16 Write your message inside.

17 **Completed** Close it back up and give it to the recipient!

## To change the Cat Message Card to a Bear Message Card

13 Start from the completed step 12 of the Cat Message Card (page 95).

14 Fold small portions of the indicated ear corners behind.

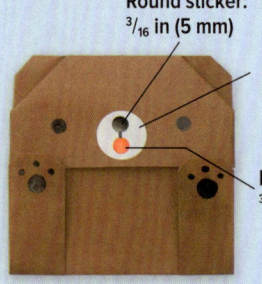
15 Apply round stickers and draw on the face and paw pads.
- Round sticker: 3/16 in (5 mm)
- Round sticker: 5/8 in (15 mm)
- Round sticker: 3/16 in (5 mm)

16 **Completed** After writing your message, it's completed!

*I'm the Bear Message Card!*

## To change the Cat Envelope to a Bear Envelope (page 94)

16 Start from step 16 of the Cat (or Bear) Envelope. (However, begin with the white side of the origami paper facing down.)

17 Fold small portions of the indicated ear corners behind.

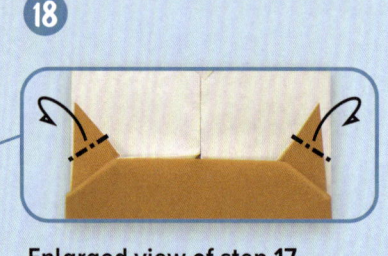
18 Enlarged view of step 17.

**Completed** Apply round stickers and draw on the face to complete.
- Round sticker: 3/16 in (5 mm)
- Round sticker: 5/8 in (15 mm)

*I'm the Bear Envelope!*

## ▶ Tatsukuri Origami is on YouTube!

Folding tutorials for the models published in this book and many others can be viewed on the YouTube channel, "Tatsukuri Origami." If there are folding passages that are difficult to understand from the book alone, please also refer to the videos on YouTube.

Please note that the folding methods or names of the models may differ slightly between the book and the videos.

https://www.youtube.com/@tatsukuriorigami